THE LITTLE

BLACK BOOK OF

MAUI &
KAUA'I

The Essential Guide to
Hawaii's Favorite Islands

JOANNE MILLER

MAPS BY DANIEL LINDROTH INC.

KE

PETER PAUPER PRESS, INC.
WHITE PLAINS, NEW YORK

DEDICATED TO MY HAWAIIAN FAMILY, THE YOUNGS:
ELEANOR, NOREEN, AND DENNIS, AND THOSE WHO HAVE
PASSED ON BUT ARE REMEMBERED WITH GREAT AFFECTION.
YOU MADE HAWAII A PLACE OF MAGIC FOR ME.

The publisher has made every effort to ensure that the content of this book was current at time of publication. It's always best, however, to confirm information before making final travel plans, since telephone numbers, Web sites, prices, hours of operation, holiday closings, and other facts are always subject to change. The publisher cannot accept responsibility for any consequences arising from the use of this book. We value your feedback and suggestions. Please write to: Editors, Peter Pauper Press, Inc., 202 Mamaroneck Avenue, Suite 400, White Plains, New York 10601-5376.

Editor: Suzanne Schwalb
Proofreader: JCommunications
Illustrations copyright © 2009 Kerren Barbas Steckler
Maps © 2009 David Lindroth Inc.
Designed by Heather Zschock

Copyright © 2009
Peter Pauper Press, Inc.
202 Mamaroneck Avenue
White Plains, NY 10601
All rights reserved
ISBN 978-1-59359-766-5
Printed in Hong Kong
7 6 5 4 3 2 1

Visit us at www.peterpauper.com

THE LITTLE
BLACK BOOK OF
MAUI &
KAUA'I

CONTENTS

INTRODUCTION

According to *Kumulipo*, an ancient creation chant, the Hawaiian Islands are the children of *Wakea* (Sky Father) and *Papa* (Earth Mother). Some say the islands are part of the sunken civilization of Mu. Mythology holds that they are also the home of mysterious sprites known as *Menehune*. Scientists say

the island chain is the product of cooled lava that emerged from volcanic vents over millions of years, and anthropologists believe Hawaii's first settlers were Polynesians who arrived in canoes with pigs, dogs, and banana and sugar cane plants. Whatever the origins of the islands and their inhabitants, Hawaii (from *Owhyhee*, the native word for "homeland") truly is a magical place.

The topography of each island is dramatically different. Volcanic peaks soar, surrounded by deeply incised valleys and steep-sided ravines sloping to shorelines, either rocky and windswept or lined with sugary beaches. (By law, there are no private beaches in Hawaii.) Miles of cultivated plantation fields lead to cooler Upcountry ranches where livestock graze contentedly. Modern cities are juxtaposed against hamlets with tin-roofed homes, wind-eroded deserts, dense jungles, and ancient lava beds—all features that make Maui, Moloka'i, Lana'i, and Kaua'i unique.

Each island was ruled independently until united by warrior King Kamehameha I in 1810. Thirty years before, England's Captain James Cook put in at a bay on what is now Kaua'i during a voyage to find the fabled Northwest Passage. He dubbed the lovely, uncharted lands  the Sandwich Isles after his patron, the Earl of Sandwich (yes, *that* Earl of Sandwich). After Cook's "discovery," traders and missionaries arrived, and Hawaii changed forever. With the end of the Hawaiian monarchy in 1893, entrepreneurs such as Sanford Dole began dividing up the countryside to farm sugarcane and pineapples, and the islands became American territory. After the 1941 attack on Pearl Harbor, Hawaii was under martial law; after the end of WWII, tourism flourished and island culture was popularized. In 1959, Hawaii became America's 50th state.

Recently, the language and traditions of ancient Hawaii have undergone a revival. Many who dwell here are *hapas* ("half this, half that") of mixed ancestry, perhaps accounting for the coexistence of peoples of multiple ethnicities (Native Hawaiian, Chinese, Japanese, Filipino, and European, among others) and for the variety of cuisines, including "new Hawaiian," which combines ethnic influences with locally sourced and organic foods.

Maui nui—"big Maui," or **Maui County**—consists of Maui, second largest island in the Hawaiian chain, Moloka'i, Lana'i, and tiny, off-limits Kaho'olawe (a former U.S. military training target now undergoing restoration).

Maui is the most developed of the islands featured in this book; the entwined cities of Kahului and Wailuku comprise its most urbanized area. Maui's famous Haleakala, "House of the Sun," is the larger of the two volcanoes that forms this island. It rises over 10,000 feet above sea level and is thought to have last erupted in 1790. Easygoing **Moloka'i**, called the most "Hawaiian" island, is known for Kalaupapa, a former colony of people afflicted with Hansen's disease, or leprosy, on its isolated northern coast. Now a state park that features some of the world's highest sea cliffs, it's only reachable by small plane, mule, or strenuous hike. Quiet **Lana'i**, once home to the largest pineapple plantation in the world, provides a serene retreat from the bustle of the bigger islands.

Lush garden isle **Kaua'i** is the oldest of the island chain. Thanks to controlled growth, there's a balance here between agribusiness and development. One of the wettest spots on Earth, it experiences an average rainfall of 460 inches. Mark Twain dubbed west Kaua'i's spectacular Waimea Canyon the "Grand Canyon of the Pacific."

HOW TO USE THIS GUIDE

We've included chapter fold-out maps with color-coded numbers that correspond to the listings in the text. **Red** listings indicate **What to See:** landmarks and attractions. **Purple** symbols show **What to Do:** beaches, tours, active experiences. **Blue** symbols indicate **Places to Eat & Drink:** restaurants, bars, and nightlife. **Orange** symbols show **Where to Shop**. And **Green** symbols tell **Where to Stay**.

Below are our keys for restaurant and hotel prices:

Restaurants

With few exceptions, the smaller ethnic restaurants found throughout Maui and Kaua'i are inexpensive and tend to be unpolished diamonds in terms of décor and service. Many grocery stores offer locally prepared food to go. Hotel restaurants charge premium prices for food, views, venues, and convenience. Our listings include addresses, phone numbers, Web sites, and hours for your travel planning convenience.

Cost of an appetizer and main course without drinks:

($)	Up to $25
($$)	$25-45
($$$)	$45-$70
($$$$)	$70 and up

DAILY GRINDS

In addition to local chains like L&L Hawaiian Barbecue and KCL Barbecue & Chinese, usually found in strip malls, *kaukau* wagons—lunch wagons parked on the street around noon and dinnertime—are favorites for good, cheap eats, or **grinds**. All serve a variety of inexpensive plate lunches and local specials to go. Things to try: salty pulled pork; chicken in sweet teriyaki sauce (sometimes barbecued on a hibachi outside the wagon's back door); *lomi lomi*, a salad with salmon or other fresh fish, tomatoes, and onions; *lau lau* ("many leaves"), the original tropical burrito: fish and pork (or beef or chicken) steamed inside an (inedible) taro leaf. Most plate lunches come with scoops of rice and macaroni salad (heavy on the mayo), and one or two entrées. Whatever you order, save room for dessert: authentic **shave ice** (no "d" on *shave*) in exotic flavors like *liliko'i* (passion fruit) and piña colada. These aren't snow cones; shaved in a special machine, the ice has an almost creamy texture. It melts quickly, but it's so delicious, it'll likely be long gone before that can happen.

Hotels

Maui and Kaua'i offer luxury accommodations with all the trimmings. Inexpensive lodgings are generally confined to hostels and camping. Guest houses—usually rooms with shared baths in private homes—are becoming difficult to find. There is pressure to make such accommodations illegal in Maui, though other islands permit them. Condo rentals are plentiful all over, however; they're an excellent budget option, since they include kitchen and often laundry facilities. But most are privately owned and vary greatly in terms of amenities and upkeep. Ask for the most updated units, and inquire about noise levels, locations, and so on, to better insure an enjoyable stay. B&Bs compare in price to condo rentals, and offer the additional fillip of a friendly face, personal recommendations, and breakfast.

Cost per night

($)	$50-125
($$)	$125-250
($$$)	$250-$400
($$$$)	$400 and up

A tip on tipping: Hawaii is the most isolated landfall in the world, and its people depend on tourist dollars for their livelihoods. Everyday goods are limited and expensive for most locals, so a little extra money slipped to guides and wait staff is not only appreciated, it's essential. Be generous.

GETTING TO MAUI & KAUA'I

Hawaiian Airlines *(800-367-5320, www.hawaiianair. com)* and a number of other carriers offer direct flights from mainland North America to Maui and Kaua'i, but

you might save a bundle by flying to O'ahu's **Honolulu International Airport (HNL)** *(300 Rodgers Blvd. #4, Honolulu, 808-836-6413, www6.hawaii.gov/dot/airports/hnl)*. Most flights make a stopover here. Then you could book a commuter flight to Maui, Moloka'i, Lana'i, or Kaua'i.

If you choose this option, you'll arrive in Hawaii at O'ahu's Overseas Terminal building and re-depart from either the Interisland Terminal building or the Commuter Terminal building. Proceed to the Commuter Terminal for **Island Air** *(800-652-6541 or 808-484-2222, www.islandair.com)*, **Pacific Wings** *(808-873-0877 or 888-575-4546, www.pacificwings.com)*, **Mokulele Airlines** *(808-426-7070 or 866-260-7070, www.mokuleleairlines.com)*, and its partner **go!** *(888-IFLYGO2 [435-9462], www.iflygo.com)*. From the Interisland Terminal, you'll take **Hawaiian Airlines** *(800-367-5320, www.hawaiianair.com)*. You can walk to either terminal in under ten minutes, or you can catch a ride on the free **Wiki Wiki** ("quick quick") **Shuttle**, which some refer to as *Wili Wili* ("twisting, turning"). Note: As of this writing, the airport is undergoing a major renovation, and air-conditioned, between-terminal "people movers" are replacing portions of the routes of the Wiki

Wiki buses, which have operated since the 1970s. Flights depart from Honolulu to Maui almost every hour, morning to evening.

When returning to the mainland via Honolulu from Maui or Kaua'i, allow at least two hours before your mainland flight leaves, as you must go through an agricultural check (for forbidden produce) in the Overseas Terminal before checking your luggage and obtaining your boarding pass. Not all inter-island carriers have luggage handling arrangements with the bigger airlines. Lines can be long.

Other "getting to" options, as well as "getting around" options, for Maui, Moloka'i, Lana'i, and Kaua'i, are listed in Chapters 1, 6, 7, and 8.

All the Hawaiian
You'll Ever Need

A visit to the islands will relax you; so will its language, which is spoken in a leisurely manner. Words can seem confusing, with only seven consonants, five vowels, an *'okina* (glottal stop), and the *kahako*, sometimes called a macron, a short line over a vowel indicating stress (which we've not used in our text, but have retained in our maps); example: *pū-pū* pronounced "poo-poo," meaning appetizers). But you'll catch on to the consistent pronunciation of vowels quickly: a (*ah*), e (*eh*), i (*ee*), o (*oh*), and u (*oo*).

All letters are pronounced, but tend to run together (except when pronounced by unhurried Hawaiians): au (*ah-oo*) becomes "ow," ia (*ee-ah*) becomes "yah," and oe (*oh-ee*) is "oy."

Most of us know that *aloha* refers to kindness, compassion, and affection; it's used for "hello," "goodbye," and in the phrase *aloha au ia 'oe* (ah-LOW-hah ow yah oy)—"I love you."

Mahalo (*mah HA low*) is "thank you," *mahalo nui* (*NEW-ee*) is "big thank you," and *mahalo nui loa*

(*LOW-ah*) is "thank you very much."

Though a few words of Hawaiian are appreciated, it's considered offensive for a *malihini* (*mah-lee-HEE-nee*)—visitor, newcomer—to attempt *da kine* (literally, "the kind"), also known as *Pidgin*, a slangy mix of languages locals reserve for themselves. But, if you get the chance, you might enjoy listening to this colorful, unofficial language. A couple of examples: "Make plate" means to get food. "Talk story" means to reminisce or swap tales.

Most locals call highways by names rather than numbers. Example: "*Honoapi'ilani* Highway" rather than "Highway 30." *Honoapi'ilani* looks daunting, but broken down, it rolls off your tongue: *Hono* (*HO-no*), *a* (*ah*), *pi'i* (*PEE*—pause for glottal stop—*ee*), *lani* (*LAH-nee*).

Hawaiian words you may hear:

'ae (*aye*) yes

'a'ole (*a-OH-lay*) no

haole (*HOW-leh*) Caucasian

heiau (*hey-EE-ow*) temple, religious site

honu (*HO-new*) endangered green sea turtle

huhu (*hoo-hoo*) angry, making a fuss

kahuna (*kah-HOO-na*) priest or expert

kai (*kigh*) ocean, sea; rhymes with *wai*, fresh water, frequently used as part of a place name

kama'aina (*ka-ma-EYE-na*) island local, often island-born

kane (*KAH-neh*) men, boys; on a restroom door, this means "Men"

keiki (*KAY-key*) child, baby—also often used to designate a beach with gentle waves

kokua (*koh-KOO-ah*) help, assistance

lolo (*low-low*) stupid

makai (*mah-KIGH*) toward the sea (used when giving directions)

manuahi (*ma-noo-AH-hee*) free, a gift

mauka (*MOW-ka*) toward the mountains (used when giving directions, as in "on the *mauka* side of the road")

'ohana (*oh-HA-na*) family

'ono (*OH-no*) the best, delicious

pau (*pow*) finished, done

pono (*POH-no*) excellent

pupule (*pah-POO-lee*) crazy

wahine (*vah-HEE-neh*) woman, also designates "Ladies" restroom

wiki (*WEE-kee*) quick, hurry

OUTDOOR RECREATION

Scuba diving, snorkeling, surfing, kite-boarding, sailing, rafting, and **swimming** may be enjoyed at dozens of beaches on each island. And Hawaii's beaches are technically accessible to all. Throughout this book, we highlight some of the top beach picks and swimming spots in Maui and Kaua'i. (Note: Many of these beaches do not have set hours, facilities, or lifeguards, and wind and water conditions may change at a moment's notice. Swim, surf, or snorkel at your own risk.) You'll find staffers at most watersports equipment rental businesses will be glad to offer recommendations of the best spots. Tour companies will take you out for a sail, a guided snorkel, or a scuba dive to uncrowded places often unreachable by other means. Excursions to **watch whales** (during the winter months) and **spot sea life** (for *honu*, turtles, and *nu'ao*, porpoise, year-round) are widely available on both Maui and Kaua'i.

Hiking is extremely popular on Haleakala Crater, in Maui, and in Waimea Canyon on Kaua'i. Hiking maps are available from visitor centers and park rangers for both these state parks. Guided tours to these and less-traveled spots are available from providers on both islands; many tours include waterfalls and swimming holes. Fit hikers may also enjoy the varied Munro Trail on Lana'i and the challenging Kalaupapa National Historic Park trail on Moloka'i. Note: Trails outside state-run areas can be primitive, root-bound, and slippery. Take care. And be aware that difficulty varies on guided hikes; what guides consider "easy" may include shifting rocks and slippery paths. Make sure your tour company knows your fitness level before you book.

Golfers will find it hard to keep their eyes on the ball for the breathtaking views from Maui and Kaua'i's spectacular golf courses. And those water hazards!

Seeing the islands on **horseback** is another great option. Stables on Maui and Kaua'i offer guided rides, and Moloka'i's famous **mules** traverse multiple switchbacks on the way to Kalaupapa *(see page 126)*.

Zip lines are one of the islands' newest form of outdoor fun: Maui and Kaua'i have multiple facilities where visitors can hike or drive in, then attach themselves to lines of varying lengths that carry them over the trees to the jungle floor below, enjoying thrilling vistas all the way. Many zip line tours include a stop at a secluded waterfall/swimming hole—sometimes with a rope swing.

State and national parks and private **campgrounds** offer a variety of terrific outdoor lodging spots, from drive-up and RV campgrounds to isolated cabins and primitive tent sites. Fees, permits, and camping requirements vary; do your research well in advance of your trip. Begin online with the Hawaii State Parks Web site (*www.hawaiistateparks.org*). Maui visitors should log on to the Haleakala National Park site (*www.nps.gov/hale*).

Maui and Kaua'i **tour companies** are generally small operations; as such, they excel in personal service and are easy to reach, especially by phone. Those with retail shops are usually open 9AM–6PM daily. Online tour booking agencies, in contrast, may not be reliable. Be sure to contact a company directly before reserving a tour. And check for online reviews of tour companies (as well as travel, dining, and lodging options) before you go.

WHEN TO VISIT

Come anytime, though if you can manage it, you'll probably enjoy an off-season visit best. Some tour companies shut down off-season, but most of the restaurants and all of the beaches are open, and the weather is great. Crowded prime tourist seasons (when many destinations and activities are heavily booked and prices are higher) are mid-December to Easter, and early June to late August. December to late April is whale-watching season, especially on Maui.

Hawaii has a remarkably stable **climate** with uniform temperatures, except at high elevations. There are two seasons: summer averages 80° F; winter drops to 73° F. Rain showers are common year round, usually during the night or morning; most—but not all—are light and brief. Each island has subregions which affect wind and rainfall. Above 3,000 feet, all bets are off; on Maui's Haleakala temps can fall below freezing.

Pack light. Bring sunscreen, insect repellent, and a sweater or windbreaker (bring seriously warmer duds if you plan to catch the sunrise at Haleakala). Otherwise, dress for tropical comfort. Many upscale restaurants allow shorts and sleeved shirts.

An island's **windward** side is open to trade winds that make it moderately rainy and cloudy (Hana, Maui, and Hanalei, Kaua'i are examples). The **leeward** side is dryer and a little warmer (like West Maui and South Kaua'i). Winds change during the year. They can be stronger from the north in winter and from the south in summer, affecting the size of waves and clarity of water. Surfers and snorkelers: Visit the Maui Weather Today link on *www.hawaiiweathertoday.com* to find out water conditions—click on "Surfing" on the left menu.

MORE VISITOR INFORMATION

Check out Hawaii's **Visitor and Convention Bureau** *(800-GOHAWAII [464-2924], www.gohawaii.com)*. Another Web site worth visiting: **Hawaii Travel Tips** *(www.travel smarthawaii.com)*, offering practical tips on what to wear, how to travel, customs, personal safety, and other topics. **Visitor bureaus** for Maui, Moloka'i, Lana'i, and Kaua'i are listed at the beginnings of Chapters 1, 6, 7, and 8.

Winter:

Lighted floats large and small come from all over Kaua'i to parade as part of the pre-Christmas **Festival of Lights** *(first Friday of December, Rice St., Lihu'e, 808-828-0014).*

★**WINTER WHALE MIGRATION** *(December–April)* makes Maui the Hawaiian Islands' top whale-watching spot. Endangered humpback whales swim 3,000 miles from Alaska to winter and calve in the warm waters of the 'Au'au ("to take a bath") Channel between Maui and Lana'i. The

TOP PICK!

Great Maui Whale Festival *(Feb., 808-249-8811, www. pacificwhale.org)* includes a Parade of Whales, a Whale Day Celebration, and other events honoring the returning behemoths. Volunteer sightings during the **Great Whale Count** *(late February)* help keep track of the giant cetaceans as they pass by the shore. The nonprofit **Pacific Whale Foundation** *(see page 109)* and other tour operators offer whale-watching cruises during the season.

Spring:

Lei **Day** *(May 1)* takes place all over Hawaii. Participants wear *leis*, make *leis*, and give away *leis*. On Maui, the **Fairmont Kea Lani hotel** *(Fairmont Kea Lani Maui, 4100 Wailea Alanui Dr., Wailea, 808-875-4100, www. fairmont.com/kealani)* displays the fragrant strings of

flowers (as well as feather and kukui nut *leis*), offers traditional entertainment, and provides a Royal Court procession with participants dressed as Hawaii's former rulers. In Kaua'i, festivities take place at the **Kaua'i Museum** *(4428 Rice St., Lihue'e, 808-245-6931, www.kauaimuseum.org)*.

Maui's **International Festival of Canoes** *(mid-May to end of May, Front St., Lahaina, 888-310-1117, www.maui festivalofcanoes.com)* commemorates Hawaiians' ties with other Pacific islanders. Native master carvers join forces with those from other parts of the Pacific to hew canoes. Visitors may attend workshops in traditional skills, such as tiki carving, old-school surfboard shaping, drum making, and house thatching. Arts displays, dance performances, traditional food, and a parade add to the fun. The festival concludes with a sunset **Launch Ceremony** at the beach.

Each island has its own version of the **Ka Hula Piko Festival** *(mid-May)*, a celebration of the hula. On Moloka'i, said to be the birthplace of the dance, festivities include entertainment, food, and crafts by local artisans *(Papohaku Beach Park, Kaluako'i, www.molokaievents. com)*. The school and dance troupe Halau Hula O Kukunaokala presents programs on the art of hula.

The colorful annual **Kaua'i Polynesian Festival** *(Memorial Day weekend; soccer field next to Vidinha Stadium, Lihu'e, 808-335-6466/5765, www.kauaipolynesianfestival.org)* begins with a Grand Polynesian *lu'au*. Festivities include

Hawaiian, Maori, Samoan, and Tahitian entertainment, Polynesian crafts, dance competitions, and more.

Summer:

The **Makawao Rodeo and Paniolo Parade** *(around the July 4 Independence Day holiday, Makawao & Olinda, Maui, www.visitmaui.com or www.makawaotowncenter.com)* celebration features traditional rodeo events and a Bull Bash (the bulls do the bashing) *(Oskie Rice Rodeo Arena, Olinda Rd., Olinda, 808-572-0386)* and a Paniolo Parade *(Baldwin & Makawao Aves., Makawao, 808-572-9565)*. During the day, competitors ride and rope for prizes; at night, they kick up their heels to country music. *Paniolo*, Hawaiian for "cowboy," is from the word for "Spanish," *español*; the first cowboys here were from Spain, Mexico, and Portugal.

Every island has a special **Independence Day** *(July 4)* celebration. In Kaua'i, an annual fundraiser for Kaua'i Hospice *(Vidinha Soccer Field, Lihu'e, 808-245-7277)* welcomes crowds to enjoy live entertainment, food, and games; it concludes with a "Concert in the Sky" aerial fireworks show.

Fall:

A celebration of the islands' medicinal and nutritional plants, the Hawaii **Healing Garden Festival** *(held throughout Hawaii; Maui's is held in September at Maui Community College, Kahului, additional tours, classes & workshops held at other locations, 808-638-0888, www.hawaiihealthguide.com)* includes a Healing Arts Fair, plus events such as cooking classes, programs on creating labyrinths and meditation gardens, organic farm tours, feng shui workshops, kids' programs, and entertainment. Hawaiian, Polynesian, Filipino, Indian/Ayurvedic, and Chinese-based philosophies are spotlighted.

Celebrating Hawaiian music, dance, and history, the **Aloha Week Festivals** *(late September–early October throughout Hawaii, 808-589-1771, www.alohafestivals. com)* aim to preserve the islands' unique traditions, with parades that showcase island flowers and colors, a costumed Royal Court, and traditional foods and entertainment.

The **Maui County Fair** *(early October, Wailuku War Memorial Complex, 1580 Ka'ahumanu Ave., Wailuku, 808-242-2721, www.mauicountyfair.com)*, Hawaii's oldest, includes 4-H competitions, homemakers' and horticulture exhibits, an Orchidland floral display, livestock, arts and crafts, treats like cotton candy and corn on the cob, as well as island food specialties, rides, "carnie" games, and entertainment.

The annual **Eo e Emalani i Alaka'i** *(October, Kaua'i, 808-335-9975, www.kokee.org)* re-enacts a royal holiday in 1871, when the islands' beloved Queen Emma (1836–1885), wife of King Kamehameha IV, trekked to Waimea Canyon and Alaka'i Swamp to take in the views. The event takes place in the meadow in front of the Koke'e Natural History Museum *(see also page 171)* and features a royal procession, hula dancing, crafts, music, and more.

TOP PICKS

TOP PICK!

Maui and Kaua'i offer one-of-a-kind attractions and experiences not to be missed! Here's a sampling:

★ Winter Whale Migration *(see page 21)*
★ Maui Ocean Center *(see page 35)*
★ Air Tour of Maui *(see page 36)*
★ Hana Highway, Maui *(see page 50)*
★ Haleakala National Park, Maui *(see page 67)*
★ Makena State Park, Maui *(see page 87)*
★ Banyan Tree, Lahaina, Maui *(see page 104)*
★ Ka'anapali Beach, Maui *(see page 107)*
★ Kalaupapa National Historic Park, Moloka'i
   (see page 126)
★ Hulopo'e Bay, Lana'i *(see page 140)*
★ Air Tours of Kaua'i *(see page 155)*
★ Waimea Canyon State Park, Kaua'i *(see page 171)*
★ Na Pali Coast, Kaua'i *(see page 185)*
★ Ke'e Beach, Kaua'i *(see page 189)*

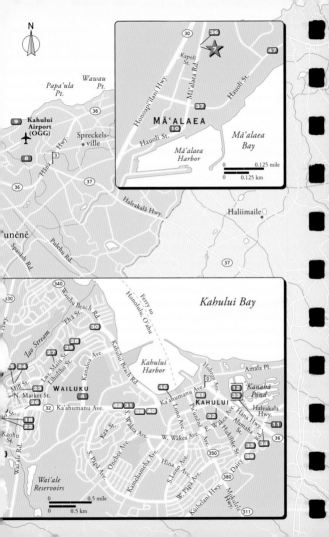

chapter 1

CENTRAL MAUI

CENTRAL MAUI

What to See:

1. 'Iao Valley State Park
2. Hawaii Nature Center
3. Kealia Pond National Wildlife Refuge
4. Maui Nui Botanical Gardens
5. Bailey House Museum
6. Alexander & Baldwin Sugar Museum
7. MAUI OCEAN CENTER ★

What to Do:

8. Blue Hawaiian Helicopters
9. Kanaha Beach Park
10. Ma'alaea Bay
11. Hawaiian Island Surf & Sport
12. Hi-Tech Surf Sports
13. Dunes at Maui Lani Golf Course
14. Kahili Golf Course
15. Maui Tropical Plantation
16. Tour-Da-Food

Places to Eat & Drink:

17. Ichiban Okazuya
18. Giannotto's
19. Maui Bake Shop
20. Café Marc Aurel
21. Takamiya Market
22. Main Street Bistro
23. Tasty Crust
24. Sam Sato's, Inc.
25. Asian Star
26. A Saigon Café
27. AK's Café
28. Home Maid Bakery
29. Tokyo Tei
30. Yakiniku Steak House and Lounge
31. Maui Culinary Academy
32. Broke da Mouth Cookie Company
33. Da Kitchen
34. Las Piñatas
35. Down to Earth Natural Foods
36. Seascape Ma'alaea Restaurant
37. Ma'alaea Waterfront Restaurant

• SNAPSHOT •

Central Maui embodies Hawaiian transitions: from city to country, development to Eden. This is the valley of the "Valley Isle," located between two inactive volcanoes. Everyone passes through here to access Maui's natural wonders, but after arriving at Central Maui's Kahului Airport, visitors may fear they've come too late: paradise has been paved and lined with parking lots, strip malls, fast-food joints, and T-shirt purveyors.

The boundaries between the towns of Kahului and Wailuku have blurred, though each retains a unique feel. Kahului is a new town, built for the growing population of visitors who fell in love with Maui and moved here. Wal-Mart, Safeway, and Costco anchor shopping centers full of goods you'd find in any mainland store. Kahului is also the home of Maui Community College. The food service program here turns out many of the island's top chefs, and treats students, locals, and visitors to excellent food. Wailuku is "Old Maui," a glimpse of what Hawaii was like before development. It's a working town of bleached, wood-frame buildings preserved with fierce pride by the community. The storefronts are home to more than 40 family businesses that have been in continuous operation for generations, including some of the best,

29

least expensive ethnic and local eateries around. Wailuku is also the jumping-off point to visit lush 'Iao Valley.

Beyond city limits, Central Maui becomes the Hawaii you've imagined. The island's main arteries take visitors through fields of dusty green sugar cane to destinations far from the madding crowds, including Ma'alena Harbor with its fabulous aquarium and wildlife refuge.

GETTING TO MAUI

By Air

Maui's **Kahului Airport (OGG)** *(1 Kahului Airport Rd., Kahului, 808-872-3893, www6.hawaii.gov/dot/airports/maui/ogg)* serves major airlines, inter-island flights, and direct flights from the mainland. You can fly direct to Kahului Airport from Los Angeles, San Francisco, Seattle, Vancouver, and other North American cities. Two smaller airports take care of commuter traffic from Kahului and Honolulu: **Kapalua-West Maui Airport (JHM)** *(access via a 2-lane road off Honoapiilani Hwy., Kapalua, 808-669-0623, www6.hawaii.gov/dot/airports/maui/jhm)* and East Maui's tiny **Hana Airport (HNM)** *(access via Alalele Pl., Hana, 808-248-8208, www6.hawaii.gov/dot/airports/maui/hnm)*. Flying to Hana from Kahului is an option if you want to avoid the long drive. You'll find more information on flying to Hawaii and Maui on page 12.

By Cruise Ship

You could also cruise to Maui. **Norwegian Cruise Lines'** ship *Pride of America* (800-327-7030, www.ncl. com) regularly anchors in

Maui's Kahului harbor. Cruise ships from **Carnival** *(888-227-6482, www.carnival.com)*, **Celebrity** *(800-647-2251, www.celebritycruises.com)*, **Holland America** *(877-724-5425, www.hollandamerica.com)*, **Princess** *(800-774-6237, www.princess.com)*, and **Royal Caribbean** *(866-562-7625, www.royalcaribbean.com)* also include ports of call in Maui. You may get a better cruise deal by consulting a cruise-only travel agency.

By Ferry

The **Hawaii Superferry** *(877-HI-FERRY or 877-443-3779, www.hawaiisuperferry.com)* offers daily service between Honolulu, Oʻahu *(corner Nimitz Hwy. & Kukahi St. at Pier 19)* and Kahului, Maui *(Kaʻahumanu Ave. bet. Puʻunene Ave. & Wharf St. at Pier 2)*. One of its advantages: You can bring a car aboard.

GETTING AROUND MAUI

Most visitors rent cars to see Maui, and major car rental companies, such as Avis and Hertz, have locations at both Kahului and West Maui airports. (Note: Rental companies usually require that you be 25 years old and have a valid driver's license and credit card.) Alternative **Word of Mouth Rent a Used Car** *(Kahului, 800-533-5929* or *808-877-2436, www.mauirentacar.com, 3-day minimum)* offers late model, air-conditioned Nissans and Toyotas with free airport pick-up and drop-off. **Maui Cruisers** *(Wailuku, 877-749-7889 or 808-249-2319, www.mauicruisers.net)* offers eight- to ten-year-old Nissan Sentras that "blend in" (for those who want to look less touristy) and get 30 to 35 miles per gallon. When driving, you'll find the islands' green roadside **mile markers** will help you find your way.

See Maui from a Harley-Davidson; rent one from **Cycle City Maui** *(150 Dairy Rd., Kahului, 808-877-7433, http://cyclecitymaui.com, M–F 8:30AM–5PM)*. You can

 also rent Harleys, Segways, cutting-edge electric cars, and exotic cars from **Aloha Toy Cars** *(640 Front St., #5, Lahaina, 888-628-4227 or 808-662-0888, www.alohatoystore.com, call for information & hours)*.

The County of Maui offers **Maui Bus** service *(808-871-4838, www.mauicounty.gov/bus)*, run by Roberts Hawaii, between central, south, west, Ha'iku, and Upcountry communities seven days a week, including holidays. The buses don't go to tourist favorite Haleakela Crater or out to Hana; however, tour company vehicles usually offer pick-up service at major hotels, so budget-minded vacationers might consider combining the two options.

SpeediShuttle's *(877-242-5777, www.speedishuttle.com)* fleet of bio-fueled Mercedes-Benz vehicles will whisk you to and from the airport, activities, and attractions.

Private charter service is also available. **Alii Cab Co.** *(808-661-3688 or 808-667-2605)* provides 24-hour taxi service. Other cab companies include **Kihei Taxi** *(808-879-3000)*, **Maui Central Cab** *(808-244-7278)*, and **Wailea Taxi** *(808-874-5000)*.

VISITOR INFORMATION

For more information, contact the **Maui Visitors Bureau** *(1727 Wili Pa Loop, Wailuku, 808-525-MAUI [6284], www.visitmaui.com, call for hours)* or the **Hawaii Visitors and Convention Bureau** *(800-GOHAWAII [464-2924], www.gohawaii.com)*.

WHAT TO SEE

A verdant basin surrounded by sheer cliffs, **ʻIao Valley State Park (1)** *(end of ʻIao Valley Rd./Hwy. 32, ʻIao Valley, www.hawaiistateparks.org/parks/maui, daily 7AM–7PM)* is the site of one of ancient Hawaiʻi's most significant battles—the defeat of Maui's armies by King Kamehameha. The iconic ʻIao Needle rises 1,200 feet from the valley floor. An easy path leads to a ridge-top lookout with views. Tips: Try to go early in the morning, before the valley is clouded. *(ʻIao, pronounced "ee-ow," means "cloud supreme.")* Mosquitoes are voracious here—make sure you're protected. While in the area (especially if you have kids), stop by **Hawaii Nature Center (2)** *(875 ʻIao Valley Rd., Wailuku, 808-244-6500, www.hawaiinaturecenter.org, daily 10AM–4PM)*. Visit its engaging

Interactive Nature Museum and take its guided **Rainforest Walk** *(M–F 11:30AM or 1:30PM, Sa–Su 11AM or 2PM)*: you'll weave through the 'Iao Valley, pass an old village site, see a *lo'i* (taro plant patch), learn about other island plants. Spectacular views of the Needle are part of the lovely ramble.

The **Kealia Pond National Wildlife Refuge (3)** *(entrance near mile marker 6, Mokulele Hwy./Hwy. 311, about 1 mile north of Kihei, 808-875-1582, www.fws.gov/pacific islands/wnwr/mkealianwr.html)*, a 691-acre wetland, is the place to spot migratory waterfowl, such as northern  pintail, alongside endangered Hawaiian stilts and coots. A boardwalk affords views of whales during the winter season. **Maui Nui Botanical Gardens (4)** *(150 Kanaloa Ave., Keopuolani Park, Kahului, 808-249-2798, www. mnbg.org, M–Sa 8AM–4PM)* is dedicated to preserving the native plants of *Maui nui* ("big Maui," or all of Maui's islands: Maui, Moloka'i, Lana'i, and Kaho'olawe).

The 1833 **Bailey House Museum (5)** *(2375-A W. Main St., Wailuku, 808-244-3326, www.mauimuseum.org; M–Sa 10AM–4PM)* showcases Hawaiian culture. Built on the site of the royal compound of the last ruling chief of Maui, the house served as the Wailuku Female Seminary for Girls until occupied by engineer, architect, and artist Edward Bailey and his family in the 1800s. The museum features paintings by Bailey, plus unique collections of land snail shells and women's hats. The surrounding gardens are filled with native and missionary-era plants, and the museum shop offers Hawaiian handicrafts, books, and gifts. Visit the **Maui Historical Society** while there, and pick up a "Discover Wailuku" walking tour map. Take your sweetie to the **Alexander & Baldwin Sugar Museum (6)** *(3957 Hansen Rd., Pu'unene, intersection of Mokulele Hwy./Rte. 311/350 & Hansen Rd., 808-871-8058, www.sugarmuseum.com, M–Sa 9:30AM–4:30PM, open Su Feb–Apr & July–Aug)*, in an historic superintendent's residence across from the still-operating sugar mill. The museum acquaints visitors with Maui's sugar heritage via photos, artifacts, working models, and interactive displays. Today, 37,000 acres of sugarcane grow on Maui's lower volcanic slopes.

TOP PICK!

One of Hawaii's top attractions, ★**MAUI OCEAN CENTER (7)** *(192 Ma'alaea Rd., Wailuku, 808-270-7000, www.mauioceancenter.com; daily 9AM–5PM, until 6PM July–Aug)* provides up-close views of hundreds of marine animals and plants, such as color-changing frogfish and black-tipped reef shark pups; more than 60 dazzling exhibits entertain and inform. A favorite: the blue-lit jellyfish tank, where ghostly jellies seem to float in space. Scuba-certified visitors over age 15 may participate in Shark Dive Maui, descending into a 750,000-gallon tank with over 20 sharks, stingrays, and thousands of tropical reef fish *($199 per person, dives on M, W, F 8:15AM)*.

WHAT TO DO

Air Tours:

For breathtaking bird's eye views of the otherworldly Haleakala Crater, the remote West Maui mountains, East Maui's magical valleys, pools, and waterfalls, and the islands beyond, don't miss taking an ★**AIR TOUR OF MAUI**. There are a variety of tours to consider. You can see Maui's beauty by helicopter, or soar over the island by plane. You can even parasail off Ka'anapali Beach. One of the top air tour operators is **Blue Hawaiian Helicopters (8)** *(1 Kahului Airport Rd., #105, Kahului, 800-745-BLUE [2583] or 808-871-8844, www.bluehawaiian.com)*, considered among Hawaii's "Ten Best of Everything" by *National Geographic*. They  offer tours of all the islands, with a variety of choices on Maui. Get a sneak peek of this unforgettable experience by viewing the video clips on the company's Web site. Its state-of-the-art choppers provide maximum visibility and you even receive a DVD of your experience.

TOP PICK!

Beaches:

Operated by the County of Maui, **Kanaha Beach Park (9)** *(behind the airport off Amala Pl., Kahului, 808-270-7389, http://hi-mauicounty.civicplus.com, daily 6:30AM–10PM, lifeguards on duty 8AM–4:30PM)* is the place to watch windsurfers and kite boarders while downing a picnic lunch. This large and well-appointed beach park has a protected swimming area, bathhouses, volleyball courts, shady areas, a lawn, and campsites *(permits required, call 808-270-7389)*.

Watersports:

Kanaha Beach Park (9) *(see above)* is the place to catch north winds; go to **Ma'alaea Bay (10)** *(south central Maui along Hwy. 31)* for winds from the south. The bay's harbor, across from **Maui Ocean Center (7)**, offers paved parking, restrooms, and picnicking. Inquire about lessons and rent equipment at **Hawaiian Island Surf & Sport (11)** *(415 Dairy Rd., Kahului, 800-231-6958, www.hawaiianisland.com, daily 8:30AM–6PM)*, catering to surfers, stand up paddle surfers, windsurfers, kite boarders, skim boarder, boogie boarders, and snorkelers. **Hi-Tech Surf Sports (12)** *(425 Koloa St., Kahului, 808-877-2111, http://htmaui. com, daily 9AM–6PM)* also offers board rentals.

Golf:

Called "a tropical-paradise layout in an Irish dunes setting" by *Golf Digest*, the **Dunes at Maui Lani Golf Course (13)** *(1333 Maui Lani Pky., Kahului, 808-873-0422, www.dunesatmauilani.com)* comprises the 18-hole championship course, restaurant, and golf school, all close to town. **Kahili Golf Course (14)** *(2500 Honoapi'ilani Hwy., Wailuku, 808-242-4653, www.kahiligolf.com)*, set along the West Maui Mountains, offers stunning vistas of the Pacific Ocean and Haleakala.

More Activities:

Take a narrated tram tour of the fields at **Maui Tropical Plantation (15)** *(1670 Honoapi'ilani Hwy./Hwy. 30, Waikapu, bet. mile markers 2 & 3, 808-244-7643, www. mauitropicalplantation.com, daily 9AM–5PM).* The 60-acre park is a working plantation that produces papaya, guava, mango, coffee, avocado, sugarcane, star fruit, and more. Want to eat like a *kama'aina* (native-born Hawaiian)? Kiss the diet good-bye and book an outing with **Tour-Da-Food (16)** *(book ahead online at www. tourdafoodmaui.com, tours meet at 8:45AM at Kepaniwai*

Park Heritage Gardens, 870 'Iao Valley Rd., Wailuku). Your host, food writer/cookbook author Bonnie Friedman, takes small groups to area eateries; dishes are served with helpings of local lore. Tours include transportation from meeting place and back, a main meal, snacks, goodie bag, and a list of additional eateries to try.

PLACES TO EAT & DRINK

Locals love the chicken katsu, teriyaki ahi, and other Japanese favorites at **Ichiban Okazuya (17) ($)** *(2133 Kaohu St., Wailuku, 808-244-7276, M–F 10AM–2PM & 4PM–7PM),* a few blocks from the Old Wailuku Inn. In the food court on Main, **Giannotto's (18) ($)** *(2050 Main St. #1A, Wailuku, 808-244-8282, M–Sa 11AM–9PM)* serves good pizza and some Italian dishes, such as lasagna and spaghetti and meatballs. The desserts are divine at **Maui Bake Shop (19) ($)** *(2092 Vineyard St., Wailuku, 808-242-0064, Su–F 6:30AM–2:30PM, Sa*

7AM–1PM) (one of the owners received culinary training in France), and soups, sandwiches, and salads are yummy, too. The place for morning espresso and evening wine and cheese is **Café Marc Aurel (20) ($)** *(28 N. Market St., Wailuku, 808-244-0852, www.cafemarc aurel.com, daily 7AM–10AM & 4PM–10PM)*. The art-filled, green-certified spot offers live entertainment a few nights a week. On your way to the beach or ʻIao Valley? Pop into **Takamiya Market (21) ($)** *(359 N. Market St., Wailuku, 808-244-3404, daily 5:30AM–6:30PM)* for a bento box lunch. **Main Street Bistro (22) ($)** *(2051 Main St., Wailuku, reservations required, 808-244-6816, M–F 11AM–7PM)* serves sophisticated comfort food, such as macadamia nut-smoked beef brisket on fresh-baked focaccia and crystallized-barbecued baby back ribs with local honey mustard, all on small plates. You might miss **Tasty Crust (23) ($)** *(1770 Mill St., Wailuku, 808-244-0845, Su, Tu–Th 6AM–10PM, F–Sa 6AM–11PM, M 6AM–3PM)* if it weren't for all the vehicles parked outside every morning. Its hot cakes (pancakes) are legendary. Owned and operated by the same family since the 1930s, **Sam Sato's, Inc. (24) ($)** *(1750 Wili Pa Loop, Wailuku, 808-244-7124, M–Sa 7AM–2PM)* is the place for pan-Asian comfort food breakfast or lunch: noodles—saimin, wonton mein, dry noodles, and chow fun—served with vegetables or without. Visitors often come to pick up *manju* (a traditional Japanese cake) to take back to the mainland. Save room for pineapple, coconut, and other fruit turnovers. Next door, **Asian Star**

(25) ($) *(1764 Wili Pa Loop, Wailuku, 808-244-1833, M–Sa 10AM–9:30PM, Su 10AM–8:30AM)* is the place to go for fresh, authentic Vietnamese. The tangerine-glazed beef is especially good. There's no sign, so **A Saigon Café (26) ($)** *(1792 Main St., Wailuku, 808-243-9560, serving lunch & dinner, call for hours)* is hard to find the first time (it's next to the only overpass in Wailuku—the only one on Maui, actually), but you'll be glad you made the

effort after tasting its home-style Vietnamese summer rolls, steaming bowls of *pho* (noodle soup) and *opakapaka* (a local fish) with ginger and garlic. The exterior of acclaimed **AK's Café (27) ($)** *(1237 Lower Main St., Wailuku, 808-244-8774, M–F 10AM–2PM & 4:45PM–8:30PM)* looks unassuming, but its chicken Marsala is nothing short of miraculous. The tiny café's prices are low, and the menu includes heart-healthy choices. Locals line up for hot *malasadas* (Portuguese donuts) at award-winning **Home Maid Bakery (28) ($)** *(1005 Lower Main St., Wailuku, 808-244-7015, http://homemaid bakery.com, daily 5–10AM & 4–10PM)*, also known for *mochi* (pounded rice with a sweet filling of red adzuki beans or white limas) and *manju* cake. The price of fresh sashimi may reach rarified heights on Maui, but not at **Tokyo Tei (29) ($)** *(1063 Lower Main St., # C101, Wailuku, 808-242-9630, http://tokyoteimaui.com, 11AM–1:30PM & 5PM–8:30PM)* in Pu'uone Plaza, serving reasonably priced sashimi for decades. The eatery also serves other Japanese fare, including tempura and teishoku trays of mixed entrées, such as teriyaki pork, shrimp, and sashimi, for lunch and dinner. **Yakiniku Steak House and Lounge (30) ($)** *(752 Lower Main St., Wailuku, 808-244-7788, 10AM–10PM)* emphasizes the "lounge" later in the evening; get there early for excellent Korean cuisine, especially beef kal-bi short ribs.

A local treasure, the **Maui Culinary Academy (31)** *(Maui Community College, 310 W. Ka'ahumanu Ave., Kahului, call ahead 808-984-3225, www.mauiculinary.com, open only during the academic year)* showcases stu-dents' expertise. Take in ocean views as you dine at its upscale **Class Act ($$)** *(808-984-3280, reservations required and cannot be made more than 7 days in advance, seatings 11AM–12:30PM during school semester)*, serving a four-course, prix fixe menu with amuse bouche, homemade bread, and iced tea and coffee for under $30 (excluding tip). The menu might include selections such as seared salmon roulade with horseradish riata and red wine Beluga lentils—and desserts such as raspberry chocolate mousse cake with dark chocolate gelato and champagne sabayon. Lucky walk-ins without reservations may snag a seat at the **Chef's Bar**. The academy's popular **Paina Food Courts ($)** *(M–F)* serve tasty, inexpensive breakfasts and lunches to students and visitors. Eateries here include **Patisserie** *(8AM–2PM)*, offering coffee and baked goods; **Campus Café** *(8AM–1PM)*, serving breakfasts, burgers, and plate lunches; **Farm to Table** *(11AM–1PM)* and **Paniolo Grill** *(11AM–1PM)*, highlighting fresh, locally grown ingredients; **Raw Fish Camp**

(11AM–1PM), sushi central; and **World Plate** *(11AM–1PM)*, satisfying diners with hearty weekly menus.

Some of Maui's best cookies, cakes, and pies are found at **Broke da Mouth Cookie Company (32) ($)** *(190 Alamaha St. #B, Kahului, 808-873-9255, M–F 6AM–7PM, Sa 7AM–5PM)*. Bring home some coconut crunch or chocolate macadamia nut cookies for a taste of the islands (if you can keep from eating them yourself). They taste so good, they "broke da mouth!" **Da Kitchen (33) ($)** *(425 Koloa St., #104, Kahului, 808-871-7782, www.da-kitchen.com, M–F 11AM–8:30PM, Sa 11AM–4PM, closed Su)* is a Maui hot spot guaranteed to leave your stomach and your wallet full. Two scoops of rice and a heaping helping of potato-mac salad accompany island favorites such as pulled pork. It's authentic local cooking at its best. Modest **Las Piñatas (34) ($)** *(395 Dairy Rd., Kahului, 808-877-8707, serving lunch & dinner)*, near a Kinko's, serves the best fish tacos on the island. Dusted with a mixture of cilantro and jalapeño, they're a spicy island version of a Mexican classic. An island-wide chain, **Down to Earth Natural Foods (35) ($)** *(305 Dairy Rd., Kahului, 808-877-2661, www.downtoearth.org, M–Sa 7AM–9PM, Su 8AM–8PM)* features produce and a by-weight salad and deli bar with lots of vegetarian items, like a tasty mock chicken salad wrap.

Spectacular views and a crowd-pleasing menu make for memorable dining at **Seascape Ma'alaea Restaurant (36)**

($) *(192 Ma'alaea Rd., Wailuku, 808-270-7000, www.mauioceancenter.com; daily 11AM–3:30PM, enter through adjacent shopping plaza for dining without aquarium admission)* at Maui Ocean Center (7). The menu includes sandwiches, salads, chicken, seafood, and desserts at reasonable prices, and the chef follows Monterey Bay Aquarium's Seafood Watch Program, serving seafood from the program's Best Choices and Good Alternatives lists.

Ma'alaea Waterfront Restaurant (37) ($$) *(50 Hau'oli St., Wailuku, 808-244-9028, www.waterfrontrestaurant.net, daily 5PM–8:30PM)* has been a destination for years for fresh-off-the-boat fish (the cioppino is a favorite) and sophisticated treatment of traditional dishes, such as beef tenderloins in a cognac demi-glace.

WHERE TO SHOP

For big-name, mainland-style shopping, try Queen Ka'ahumanu Center (38) *(275 W. Ka'ahumanu Ave., Kahului, Ste. 1200, 808-877-3369, www.queenkaahumanucenter.com, M–Sa 9:30AM–9PM)* and Maui Marketplace (39) *(270 Dairy Rd./Hwy. 380, Kahului, hours vary by store)*.

For authentic local shopping, pick up honey and *liliko'i* (passion fruit; it's like lemon with a twist) products at the Maui's Fresh Produce Farmer's Market (40) *(center stage area, Queen Ka'ahumanu Center, 275 W. Ka'ahumanu Ave., Kahului, 808-298-4289, Tu–W, F*

7AM–4PM) or Maui Mall Farmer's Market & Craft Fair (41) *(Maui Mall, 70 E. Ka'ahumanu Ave., Kahului, 808-871-1307, Tu–W, F 7AM–4PM)*, and check out the Maui Swap Meet (42) *(Maui Community College, 310 Ka'ahumanu Ave., Kahului 808-877-3100, Sa 7AM–noon)* for a weird, wild assortment of new and used goods.

Stroll North Market Street (43) *(Wailuku, hours vary by store)* and discover some of the island's oldest shops, packed with treasures. One of the most irresistible: **Brown & Kobayashi** *(38 N. Market St., Wailuku, 808-242-0804, call for hours)*, specializing in gorgeous Asian antiques and *objets d'art*.

On the way to or from the 'Iao Needle, Tropical Gardens of Maui (44) *(200 'Iao Valley Rd., Wailuku, 808-244-3085, www.tropical gardensofmaui.com, daily 9AM–5PM)* is a botanical garden and export nursery featuring exotic orchids and tropical plants from all parts of the world. Take a self-guided tour of the garden, koi pond, and palm grotto—picnic tables are available for lunching under the fronds. The nursery will ship plants home for you.

WHERE TO STAY

Get a glimpse of 1920s–1930s Maui at gracious Old Wailuku Inn at Ulupono (45) **($$)** *(2199 Kaho'okele St., Wailuku, 808-244-5897, www.mauiinn.com)*, located in Wailuku's historic district, a short walk from shops and eateries. Stay in one of ten lovely rooms, either in its main house or in the inn's "Vagabond's House," named after "vagabond" Hawaiian poet laureate Don Blanding (1894–1957). Each room is dedicated to a flower named in Blanding's poem "Old Hawaiian Garden." All rooms have private baths and include breakfast.

Maui Seaside Hotel (46) ($-$$) *(100 W. Ka'ahumanu Ave., Kahului, 800-560-5552, www.mauiseasidehotel.com)* is a clean, quiet, motel/hotel with the usual amenities. The two-story spot has a restaurant, pool, and breeze-catching *lanai*/balcony. If you need to stay near the airport, this is the place.

For a tranquil stay on Maui's south shore near **Maui Ocean Center (7)**, consider renting a condominium on Ma'alaea Bay. (There are no hotels.) **Ma'alaea Bay Realty & Rentals ($-$$) (47)** *(280 Hau'oli St., Ma'alaea Village, Wailuku, 800-367-6084, www.maalaeabay.com)* rents oceanfront and oceanview one-, two-, and three-bedroom condos with kitchens in Ma'alaea Bay Village.

Central Maui has three hostels; the best by far is **Banana Bungalow ($) (48)** *(310 N. Market St., Wailuku, 800-846-7835, www.mauihostel.com)*, offering dorm-style rooms and private rooms, and discounted monthly rates (with specials for surfers with gear). The hostel boasts a one-acre tropical garden with hot tub, lounge, kitchen, game room, community TV, coin laundry, pay phones, free Internet, beach and airport shuttles, and free tours. Make no mistake: the hostel caters to students, surf bums, and older, budget-minded travelers, but it offers outstanding value.

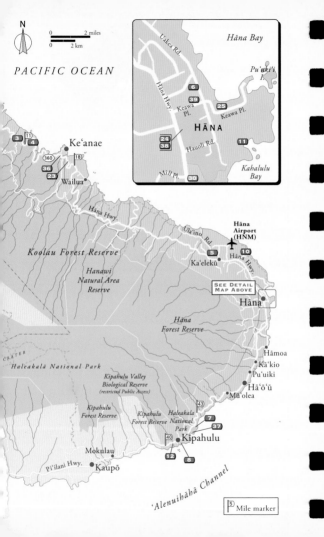

N

PACIFIC OCEAN

0 — 2 miles
0 — 2 km

Ke'anae

360
18
36
23
Wailua

3
11
4

Hāna Hwy.

Koolau Forest Reserve

Hanawi Natural Area Reserve

'Ula'ino Rd.

Hāna Airport (HNM)

5
Ka'elekū
10
Hāna Hwy.

SEE DETAIL
MAP ABOVE

Hāna

Hāna Forest Reserve

CRATER

Haleakala National Park

Kipahulu Valley Biological Reserve
(restricted Public Access)

Hāmoa
Ka'kio
Pu'uiki
Hā'ō'ū
Mu'olea

Kīpahulu Forest Reserve

Kipahulu Forest Reserve

Haleakala National Park

43

7
37

Mokulau
40
12   8
Kīpahulu

Pi'ilani Hwy.   Kaupō

'Alenuihāhā Channel

5   Mile marker

Detail map:

'Uakea Rd.

Hāna Bay

Hāna Hwy.

Keawa Pl.

6
39
25

Pu'uki'i I.

Keawa Pl.

HĀNA

24
38

Hauoli Rd.

11

Mill Pl.

30

Kahalulu Bay

EAST MAUI

Pauwela Pt.

SEE DETAIL MAP BOTTOM

9
2

Ku'au

29
9
Hāna Hwy.
Lower
Pā'ia

Hāmākua
Poko

36
Pauwela

35
Holokai Rd.

SEE DETAIL MAP BELOW

Ha'ikū

Ulumalu

Kaupakulua

Huelo

360
5
Hāna Hwy

Pā'ia

Kailua

37

Kaheka
Village

Kailua Village

Kokomo Rd.

Kuhikoa Rd.

Kokomo

Ka'ili'ili

Makawao
Forest Reserve

36

Pua Koa Pl.

PAUWELA

36
34

W. Kuiaha Rd.

21

Ha'ikū Rd.

Kaupakalua Rd.

Ha'ikū Rd.

Kaupakulua Rd.

20
32

HA'IKŪ

378

23

Kokomo Rd.

19
33

Poho Pl.
Kaiholo Pl.

KŪ'AU

Kaimao St.

Ka'iani Rd.

HALEAKALĀ

36

Kulani Pl.

Kahikinui
Forest Reserve

31
32

Hāna Hwy.

Lwr. Hāmākuapoko Rd.

Loio Pl. Kuipoho

15
29
16
17

LOWER
PĀ'IA

Baldwin Ave.

13
14

18

chapter 2

EAST MAUI

EAST MAUI

What to See:
1. HANA HIGHWAY ★
2. Ho'okipa Beach Park
3. Garden of Eden Arboretum & Botanical Garden
4. Kaumahina State Wayside
5. Ka'eleku Caverns
6. Hana Cultural Center & Museum
7. 'Ohe'o Gulch
8. Palapala Ho'omau Congregational Church

What to Do:
9. H. A. Baldwin Park
10. Wai'anapanapa State Park
11. Kaihalulu Beach
12. Maui Stables

Places to Eat & Drink:
13. Shave Ice
14. Flatbread Company
15. Ono Gelato Company
16. Paia Fish Market
17. Cafe Mambo
18. Fresh Mint
19. Mama's Fish House
20. Hana Hou Café
21. Pauwela Café & Bakery
22. Fukushima's Store
23. Halfway to Hana
24. Ka'uiki
25. Tutu's Snack Shop

Where to Shop:
26. Maui Crafts Guild
27. Ha'iku Marketplace
28. Ha'iku Town Center
29. Pa'uwela Cannery
30. Hasegawa General Store

Where to Stay:
31. Spyglass House
32. Blue Tile Beach House
33. Inn at Mama's Fish House
34. Pu'u Koa Maui Rentals
35. Maui Ocean Breezes
36. YMCA Camp Keanae
10. Wai'anapanapa State Park
37. Haleakala National Park Kipahulu Campground
38. Hotel Hana-Maui & Honua Spa
39. Aloha Cottages

★ *Top Picks*

● SNAPSHOT ●

The east side of Maui is home to two historic villages: the old sugar-cane boomtown of Pa'ia *(www.paiamaui. com)* and former cannery town Ha'iku. Both are stops along one of the island's most scenic—and challenging—attractions: the winding road to Hana and beyond. Following the trail of an ancient footpath, Hana Highway (few refer to it by its official name of Route 36) hugs the rugged northeast coast of Maui, the windward side of the island. Because of the region's relative isolation, travelers venturing here may truly experience an "Eden-esque" side of Maui.

The Hana Highway passes through northern Lower Pa'ia on the island's northern coast. Surrounded by cane fields, this funky bohemian village was once a booming plantation town. Today, the three-block-long commercial stretch just off the highway is packed with vibrant storefronts, galleries, boutiques, and several notable restaurants. Upper Pa'ia, mostly residential, is a little farther south ("upper" and "lower" always refer to height and placement on the mountain; "lower" is always closer to the shore). Continuing east on the Hana Highway, a right turn on Ha'iku Road (Route 398) leads to the quiet hamlet of Ha'iku. For much of the 20th century, Ha'iku's townspeople processed and shipped pineapples and guavas from local canneries. Ha'iku also served as a WWII Marine base. Of late, the huge cannery buildings have found new life; they're filled with eateries, studios, and shops. Note: Ha'iku Road veers sharply to the east in the middle of town and the straight road continues on as Kokomo Road/Route 398; this is a source of much confusion.

After leaving Ha'iku, visitors return to the Hana Highway to continue on through paradise to the ancient village of Hana. Many opt to stay overnight in this low-key hamlet, a far cry from commercial, crowded Maui. Hana was once known for it sugar plantations, but by 1944, the area became a huge cattle ranch developed by Paul Fagan, owner of the San Francisco Seals baseball team; spring training was held here in 1946. In April of that year, a tsunami destroyed many homes on the Hana coast; afterward, the village was reborn in smaller size. Today Hana welcomes those who appreciate its remoteness, exclusivity, and old-fashioned sense of *aloha*.

Beyond Hana is Kipahulu, the coastal far side of Haleakala National Park. Hiking and swimming among freshwater pools are popular pastimes, and a local stable offers Hawaiian culture along with its trail treks.

WHAT TO SEE

Called the highway to Heavenly Hana, the King's Highway, and one of the world's top scenic drives, the ★HANA HIGHWAY (1) *(Hwy. 36 & Hwy. 360)* is the breathtaking road from central Maui's Kahului to far-flung Hana on the island's eastern end. The picturesque journey itself is the main attraction, but the first thing to consider when attempting the famous road trip is that the twisty thoroughfare comprises hundreds of often-blind hairpin turns, heavy traffic, sheer cliffs, and several dozen one-lane bridges. The distance is 68 miles, but the drive can easily take three hours! If you do drive, plan ahead. Start out early in the morning and make a day of it. Call 808-986-1200 to check on road conditions. Bring food, water, insect repellant, towels, your camera, and a detailed road map that lists all the waterfalls and other sights. (We highlight a number of "must-sees" throughout this chapter.) Fill your tank with gas. Take your time, stop often, and let faster motorists pass. Locals will likely give you a couple of friendly toots on the horn as they go by. Be aware that in many places, speeds drop to 10 miles per hour. Want to leave the driving to someone else? Take a van or coach tour. Those who suffer from motion sickness might want to fly *(commuter flights to Hana leave from Kahului airport; see "Getting to Maui" on page 30).* "Flatlanders" sometimes find it easier to drive at night, when other vehicles' approaching headlights indicate the locations of the switchbacks ahead. But daytime drivers

TOP PICK!

get to enjoy unforgettable sights: pristine waterfalls, ethereal rainforests, colorful enclaves lined with fresh fruit stands, and spectacular ocean vistas.

See top surfers in action at Ho'okipa Beach Park (2) *(mile marker 9, Hana Hwy./Hwy. 36, Paia, 572-8122, www.co.maui. hi.us/parks/maui/east/Hookipa BeachPark.htm, lifeguard on duty*  *8AM–4:30PM)*, east of **Pa'ia**, the "Windsurfing Capital of the World." Competition-level windsurfers, kite surfers, and long board riders surf here all year, but big 10- to15-foot swells make the beach a magnet for elite performers in winter. The Aloha Classic and Red Bull surfing competitions and the Maui Sports Foundation events are held here. Surfing is limited to expert level when the waves pound, but the beach has a one-eighth-mile-long coral reef that protects a pond-like area perfect for summer and early morning swimming.

Garden of Eden Arboretum & Botanical Garden (3) *(past mile marker 10, 10600 Hana Hwy./Hwy. 360, 808-572-6453, daily 8AM–3PM)* is a pleasant stop between the village of Kailua and Ke'anae. You may walk, picnic, and even drive through its 26 acres of carefully cultivated tropical trees and flowers; hundreds of plants are identified with labels. One trail here leads to a **Puohokamoa Falls** overlook. Feed the ducks and peacocks, or stop by the solar-powered gift shop, offering crafts and other items made by locals. Continue on, approaching mile

51

marker 11, where you'll spot a turnaround; there's a short trail here along the canyon (watch your step!) that leads to a wonderful view of **Lower Puohokamoa Falls**.

Kaumahina State Wayside (4) *(after mile marker 12, Hana Hwy./Hwy. 360, www.hawaiistateparks.org/parks/maui/ kaumahina.cfm, daily 6AM–6PM)* is an excellent spot to pull over, stretch your legs, and take in spectacular lush green vistas down the coast to the volcanic Ke'anae Peninsula and back into Ke'anae Valley, the largest on the north side of Haleakela Crater. A little further on, Ke'anae Village *(end of Ke'anae Rd.)* is a private residential and agricultural area. *Kapu* ("forbidden") signs keep tourists at bay.

Molten lava takes on many forms; one of the most interesting is the **lava tube**, a hollow structure that can be as small as a tree trunk or as large as a cave. A prime example: the mammoth Ka'eleku Caverns (5) *(turn left on 'Ula'ino Rd. past mile marker 31 on Hana Hwy./Hwy. 360)*. Visitors may access the cavern, filled with stalactites, stalagmites, and other fascinating formations, via a 40-minute self-guided tour through **Maui Cave Adventures** *(205 'Ula'ino Rd., Hana, 808-248-7308, www.mauicave.com, M–Sa 10:30AM–3:30PM, some Su, call ahead)*.

Explore Hana's past at the Hana Cultural Center & Museum (6) *(4974 Uakea Rd., Hana, 808-248-8622, www.hookele.com/hccm, daily 10AM–4PM)*, near the **Hana Beach Park** entrance. Especially fine are the Hawaiian quilts. You'll also find a variety of artifacts, the historic

Hana courthouse and "lock-up," as well as re-creations of thatched Hawaiian *hales*, or huts: one for cooking, one for meeting, one for sleeping, and one for building dugout canoes.

About nine miles beyond Hana, you'll find the lovely pools of 'Ohe'o Gulch (7) *(in Kipahulu, about 9 miles beyond Hana, Hana Hwy./Hwy. 31, www.nps.gov/hale/planyourvisit/kipahulu.htm, open 24 hrs)*, sometimes referred to as the **Seven Sacred Pools** (though there are actually more than 24). Warning: Visitors hike and swim in this isolated area at their own risk. The pools and the waterfalls that form them are irresistible swim-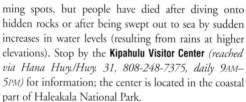ming spots, but people have died after diving onto hidden rocks or after being swept out to sea by sudden increases in water levels (resulting from rains at higher elevations). Stop by the **Kipahulu Visitor Center** *(reached via Hana Hwy./Hwy. 31, 808-248-7375, daily 9AM–5PM)* for information; the center is located in the coastal part of Haleakala National Park.

The cemetery behind quaint Palapala Ho'omau Congregational Church (8) *(at the 41 mile marker, S. Hana Hwy./Hwy. 31, Kipahulu)* is the final resting place of air pioneer Charles Lindbergh (1902–1974), the first man to fly solo across the Atlantic. Lindbergh spent his last years in Hana. Be respectful when visiting. You may park and picnic in tiny **Kipahulu Point Park** *(mile 44, Hana Hwy./Hwy. 31, Kipahulu, 808-*

248-7022, http://mauicounty.gov/parks/maui/Hana/ KipahuluPointLightStn.htm) next door, overlooking the ocean.

WHAT TO DO
Beaches:
H. A. Baldwin Park (9) *(mile marker 6, Hana Hwy., www.co.maui.hi.us)* next to Maui Country Club just to the east of Pa'ia, is a pleasant park offering sandy-beach swimming (with lifeguard on duty), grills, picnic tables, and restrooms. It's a popular spot for families to spend the day. Note: Occasional car break-ins are reported here; lock valuables in the trunk. Three miles before Hana village, turn down the clearly marked road to **Wai'anapanapa State Park (10)** *(end of Wai'anapanapa Rd. off Hana Hwy./Hwy. 360, mile marker 32, Hana, 808-244-4354, www.hawaiistateparks.org/parks/maui/ waianapanapa.cfm, open daily, tent camping by reservation only; visit Web site for details).* This is a wild and spectacular park. Its **black sand beaches** were formed by molten lava of long ago that shattered upon contact with the water; over the years, waves smashed the volcanic rocks to grains of sand. The park also boasts a native forest, a stone arch, underwater caves, blowholes, a seabird colony, and the remains of a *heiau* (native place

of worship). One trail leads to a lighthouse with broad views. Tip: Hiking is challenging; wear sturdy, non-slip, closed shoes. This is a beautiful place to snorkel (*Wai'anapanapa* means "glistening waters"), but make sure you get out in the morning or when the water is calm—the hard, sharp lava and heavy surf may harm an unwary swimmer. When in doubt, stay on the shore and simply enjoy the seascape. Unique **Kaihalulu Beach (11)** *(end of Uakea Rd., Hana)* is also known as **Red Sand Beach** for its red cinder sand. The beach is surrounded by rough, slippery terrain and private property, making it largely inaccessible; take advantage of a Maui air tour *(see page 36)* to view its beauty.

More Activities:

Maui Stables (12) *(just past mile marker 40, Hwy. 37, Kipahulu, 808-248-7799, www.mauistables.com, 2 rides daily, check-ins at 9:30AM & 1PM, reserve in advance, refreshments included)* isn't just a ride in the park. This native-owned company employs young locals who love what they do. Riders are invited to take part in the true spirit of the islands. Guided rides wind through spectacular scenery while visitors are immersed in Hawaiian history and spirituality. Many say this is the high point of their trip to Maui. Make plenty of time to get there; to check on road conditions call the stables or call 808-986-1200.

PLACES TO EAT & DRINK

Pining for a plate lunch? **Shave Ice (13) ($)** *(77 Hana Hwy./Hwy. 36, Pa'ia, 808-579-8747, daily 11AM–5:30PM)* is a good choice. Folks also stop by for shave ice, of course, and cold drinks. Out-of-the-ordinary pizza joint **Flatbread Company (14) ($)** *(89 Hana Hwy./Hwy. 36, Pa'ia, 808-579-8989, flatbreadcompany.com, daily 11:30AM–10PM)* works magic with organic produce and free-range and nitrate-free meats. Pies come with the usual favorite toppings, as well as local specialties such as goat cheese and smoked pork, and are baked in a handmade wood-burning earthen oven.

Kula strawberry. *Liliko'i.* Ferrero Rocher. Moonlight on the Grove. With flavors like these, **Ono Gelato Company (15) ($)** *(115D Hana Hwy./Hwy. 36, Pa'ia, 808-579-9201, www.onogelatocompany.com, daily 11AM–10PM)* truly lives up to its name, which means "delicious." Nearly half its selection (with ingredients sourced locally and organic, if possible) is dairy-free. Popular **Pa'ia Fish Market (16) ($)** *(100 Hana Hwy./Hwy. 36, Pa'ia, 808-579-8030, www.paiafishmarket.com, daily 11AM–9:30PM)* transforms local catches into perfect fish burgers, accompanied by tartar sauce, coleslaw, tomato, and cheese. And prices are so easy on the wallet many visitors return nearly every day. Though crowded at lunchtime, it's worth the wait. **Cafe Mambo (17) ($)** *(30 Baldwin Ave, Pa'ia, 808-579-8021, www.cafemambomaui.*

com, daily 8AM–9PM) serves a tasty salad of crispy *kalua* duck (cooked in an underground oven) with soy/orange/honey glaze, and smoked bacon and mango salsa. Vegetarian entrées such as ginger sesame tofu burger and spinach nut falafel are also winners. In addition, the café turns out picnic/box lunches, with offerings such as sandwiches, chips, brownies, and soft drinks. Unpretentious eatery **Fresh Mint (18) ($)** *(115 Baldwin Ave., Pa'ia, 808-579-9144, daily 5PM–9PM)* serves a vegan Vietnamese menu that will tickle your tastebuds with unexpected variety. The soups, spring rolls with peanut sauce, and pad Thai are of particular note. **Mama's Fish House (19) ($$)** *(799 Poho Pl., Pa'ia, 808-579-8488, www.mamasfishhouse.com, daily 11AM–9PM)* is as much an institution as the palm trees that dot its beach. The fish dishes here are consistently tasty and beautifully prepared, portions are generous, and service is top-notch. Reserve ahead and request a window table to watch the sunset.

Ha'iku locals and visitors in the know eat at the **Hana Hou Café (20) ($)** *(Ha'iku Marketplace #404, 810 Ha'iku Rd., Ha'iku, 808-575-2661, www.hanahoucafe.com, daily 5:30PM–9PM, live music M, W–Sa)*. The casual atmosphere belies its excellent burgers, quesadillas (crab is especially good), and grilled fish. A varied American menu pleases the *keiki* (kids). **Pauwela Café & Bakery (21) ($)** *(375 W. Kuiaha Rd., #37, Ha'iku, 808-575-9242, www.pauwelacafe.com, daily 6AM–2PM, dine in M–F*

7AM–1PM), in the Pa'uwela Cannery (29) serves a much broader menu than pastries and coffee, and the place is known for its friendly, "true aloha" spirit. Stop by here for a sweet and a last caffeine jolt before returning to the Hana Highway. **Fukushima's Store (22) ($)** *(815 Ha'iku Rd., Ha'iku, 808-575-2762, M–Sa 6:30AM–8PM, Su 6:30AM–5PM)* has been around for decades, and is a good place to pick up drinks, snacks, produce, and some staples. The store's claim to fame is its hot dogs—people travel for miles to down a red hot from this little market.

Beyond mile marker 17 on the Hana Highway, **food and fruit stands** pop up like mushrooms after a rain. Some are on the honor system—take what you want and leave the money. Many serve sandwiches and shave ice, as well as fresh fruit and drinks. One of the stands, **Halfway to Hana (23) ($)** *(1/3 mile past mile marker 17, Hana Hwy./Hwy. 360, Ke'anae, no phone)* (actually more than halfway) has been around for more than 20 years and is known for its banana bread.

In Hana, **Ka'uiki (24) ($$)** *(Hotel Hana-Maui, 5031 Hana Hwy./Hwy. 36, Hana, 808-248-8211 or 800-321-4262, www.hotelhanamaui.com, daily 7AM–10PM)* serves breakfast, lunch, and dinner; the menu, which changes daily, depending on freshness and availability, is a blend of regional and Pacific Island cuisine. Dress up a bit for dinner (men, no tank tops, but dress shorts are OK). Come Fridays for a Hawaiian buffet and performances by local musicians *(F 6PM–9PM; show starts at 7PM; reservations required)*. Hana's **Tu Tu's Snack Shop ($) (25)** *(Hana Beach Park, Hana, M–Sa 8AM–4PM)* sells breakfast and lunch items on the waterfront, including French toast, plate lunches, burgers, and noodle plates.

WHERE TO SHOP

The intersection of Hana Highway and Baldwin Avenue in colorful, laid-back **Pa'ia** is home to an array of small shops selling food, clothing, sporting goods, and more. This is a great place to stroll and people-watch. Maui Crafts Guild (26) *(69 Hana Hwy., Pa'ia, 808-579-9697, www.mauicraftsguild.com, daily 10AM–6PM)*, is owned and operated by resident artisans.  As much as possible, they use local, natural materials in creating their high-quality, reasonably priced work; if you're shopping for art to take home, this is the place.

In **Ha'iku**, former pineapple and guava canneries are being transformed into collections of shops, dining spots, and artists' studios. The Ha'iku Marketplace (27) *(810 Ha'iku Rd., Ha'iku)* contains a grocery, laundromat, and eateries. The Ha'iku Town Center (28) *(813 Kokomo Rd., Ha'iku)* has a café, bakery, restaurants, and more. Pa'uwela Cannery (29) *(375 W. Kuiaha Rd., Ha'iku)* is home to **Pauwela Café and Bakery (21)** *(see above)* and a buzzing art space known as **DaFactory** *(808-575-9222, www.mauiglassblowing.com)*. Here, artists create large-scale glass work and host live events and parties, including events where international chefs incorporate glassworking with food creation. Woodworkers, surfboard shapers, and others also make the former cannery their base.

Hana's famous Hasegawa General Store (30) *(5165 Hana Hwy./Hwy. 360, Hana, 808-248-7079 or 808-248-8231, M–Sa 7AM–7PM, Su 8AM–6PM)* is an old-fashioned, one-stop shop for everything under the sun, from soft drinks to hardware and household items. Its ATM is the east coast's only one.

WHERE TO STAY

Note: Most accommodations listed here require minimum stays. Spyglass House (31) ($$) and sister property **Dolphin House** ($) *(both located at 367 Hana Hwy./Hwy. 36, Pa'ia, 808-579-8608 or 800-475-6695, www.spyglassmaui.com)* are three-bedroom waterfront houses a half-mile from Pa'ia. Individual rooms may be reserved,

or either of the houses may be rented separately. Each house contains a full kitchen, an oceanfront living room, and a *lanai* deck overlooking the sea. Self-serve breakfast coffee, tea, juice, waffles, bagels, and English muffins are provided in both properties. Nearby

Blue Tile Beach House (32) ($$-$$$) *(459 Hana Hwy./Hwy. 36, Pa'ia, 808-579-6446, www.beachvacationmaui.com)* is a 5,000-square-foot, six-bedroom beachfront home with two spiral stairways leading to separate wings. One wing features two oceanfront suites with *lanais* and kitchenettes; the other has four private bedrooms with common kitchen, dining, and entertainment spaces. Rooms may be rented individually or one may rent the entire house.

Accommodations at the **Inn at Mama's Fish House (33)** **($$-$$$)** *(799 Poho Pl., Pa'ia, 808-579-9248, www.mamas fishhouse.com)* include honeymoon-worthy beachfront cottages decked out in retro Polynesian style, complete with *lanais* from which to catch those amazing sunsets. The inn's garden cottages with private patios range from studios to two-bedroom units and are less expensive.

Pu'u Koa Maui Rentals (34) ($) *(66 Pu'u Koa Pl., Ha'iku, 808-573-2884, www.puukoa.com)* offers affordable and spacious studios and one-bedroom apartments in two private houses in a quiet neighborhood five minutes from Ho'okipa Beach. The units feature TVs, microwaves, coffee makers, toaster ovens, hot plates, dishes, and a small refrigerator, along with private baths. Five-night minimum. Privately owned **Maui Ocean Breezes (35) ($$)** *(240 N. Holokai Rd., Ha'iku, 808-572-2775, www.mauivacationhideaway.com)* consists of three fully equipped rental units and a 40-foot saltwater swimming pool, lush grounds, and views of the ocean and Haleakala. Rentals include the Whispering Bamboo cottage, Hibiscus Hideaway apartment, and the Swaying Palms studio. All are rented by the week.

Halfway to Hana, **YMCA Camp Keanae (36) ($)** *(13375 Hana Hwy./Hwy. 360, Ke'anae, 808-248-8355, www. mauiymca.org)* provides great views and terrific options for campers, including cottage, cabin, and dorm-style accommodations, tent camping, and facilities for group get-togethers. There are two fire pits and bathhouses with hot showers.

Wild **Wai'anapanapa State Park (10)** *(end of Wai'anapanapa Rd. off Hana Hwy./Hwy. 360, mile marker 32, Hana, www. hawaiistateparks.org/parks/maui/ waianapanapa.cfm)* offers spots for tent camping and a few cabins that sleep up to six. Though not on the beach, the cabins are popular. Reserve camp or cabin permits in advance *(follow directions on Hawaii State Parks Web site: www.hawaiistateparks.org/camping/fees.cfm, or call 808-587-0300 M–F 8AM–3:30PM Hawaii time)*.

Beyond Hana, you'll find tent sites with breathtaking cliff views *(available on a first-come first-serve basis)* at the **Haleakala National Park Kipahulu Campground (37)** *(S. Hana Hwy./Hwy. 31 to the Kipahulu coastal area of Haleakala National Park near 'Ohe'o Gulch, campsites one mile south of Kipahulu Visitor Center, 808-248-7375, www.nps.gov/hale/planyourvisit/kipahulu.htm)*, but this is roughing it: you must bring your own water and be prepared for rain, harsh sun, and mosquitoes. The campground has picnic tables, grills, and pit toilets. No permits required, but there is a park entry fee. See national park Web site for details.

In Hana, on the other end of the spectrum, **Hotel Hana-Maui & Honua Spa (38)** (**$$$-$$$$**) *(5031 Hana Hwy./ Hwy. 360, Hana, 808-248-8211 or 800-321-HANA [4262], www.hotelhanamaui.com)* offers sea ranch and bay cottages, starting at $495 a night, and a Plantation House on four acres for $4,000 a night. This AAA, four-diamond award-winning resort comes with a *Travel & Leisure* top-rated spa, complimentary beach shuttle, morning yoga classes, two swimming pools, free bicycle use—the list goes on. It's a first-class experience in this lush, unspoiled area.

Privately-owned **Aloha Cottages (39)** (**$**) *(83 Keawa Pl., Hana, 808-248-8420)* can be a potential bargain for those seeking no-frills lodging in Hana. You may want to see the accommodations first. Warning: The host will not tolerate late checkouts.

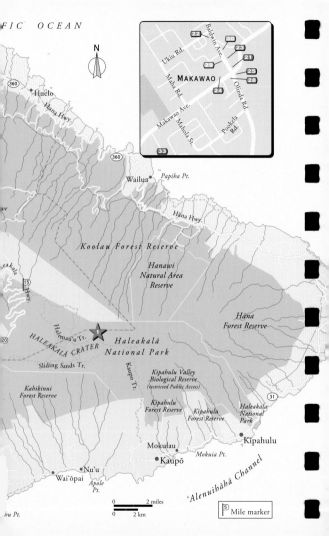

chapter 3

UPCOUNTRY MAUI

UPCOUNTRY MAUI

What to See:

1. HALEAKALA NATIONAL PARK★
2. Haleakala Sunrise
3. Holy Ghost Catholic Church
4. Hui No'eau Visual Arts Center

What to Do:

1. Haleakala National Park
5. Hike Maui
6. Polipoli Spring State Recreation Area
7. Maui Downhill
8. Haleakala Bike Company
9. Pi'iholo Ranch
10. Haleakala on Horseback
11. Makena Stables
12. O'o Farm
13. Ali'i Kula Lavender Farm
14. Shim Farm
15. Kula Botanical Gardens
16. Sunrise Country Market & Protea Farm
17. Enchanting Floral Gardens
18. Surfing Goat Dairy Farm
19. Tedeschi Vineyards

Places to Eat & Drink:

20. Hali'imaile General Store
21. T. Komoda Store & Bakery
22. Café del Sol
23. Café O'Lei
24. Down to Earth Natural Foods
25. Polli's Mexican Restaurant
26. Kula Lodge and Restaurant
27. Ulupalakua Ranch Deli and Grill
28. Casanova Italian Restaurant & Deli

Where to Shop:

29. Hot Island Glass
30. Aloha Cowboy
31. Kula Marketplace
32. Ulupalakua Ranch Store

Where to Stay:

33. Hale Ho'okipa Inn
34. Olinda Country Cottages and Inn
26. Kula Lodge and Restaurant
1. Haleakala National Park
6. Polipoli Spring State Recreation Area

• SNAPSHOT •

When the beach sun gets too strong, head for misty-cool Upcountry. The village of Makawao, gateway to the region, remains less affected by development than Maui's coastal communities—except for one of the best

nightclubs on the island and two great cafés. Since the late 19th century, horseback-riding *paniolo* have been wrangling cattle here in wide-open upland fields. The Makawao Rodeo, held on July 4th, is Hawaii's largest *paniolo* competition.

The Kula Highway is the route to agri-tourist farms offering tours, flowers, and produce, to Kula town itself, and to the immense 'Ulupalakua cattle ranch and Tedeschi Winery. Residential yards lining the west side of the Kula Highway (Highway 37 or *old* Haleakela Highway) look like botanical gardens gone wild. A drive down pretty side streets will reveal bounties of fruit and flowers for sale near residents' mailboxes, payable on the honor system. It also affords some of the most incredible views of Maui, the partially submerged Molokini crater, and the island of Lana'i. In early May, flowering jacaranda trees bloom, giving the color purple new meaning. The highway continues around the south coast of Maui, but becomes unpaved and stops just short of the east side village of Kaupo. On most maps, the road is renamed Pi'ilani Highway or Highway 31 after passing 'Ulupalakua—the same name as another road that runs beyond Makena to the west. The roads were once meant to be connected, but it hasn't happened.

Highway 377 (the *new* Haleakala Highway) is the "direct" route to the west side of a geological wonder sacred to ancient Hawaiians: Haleakala Crater. *Haleakala* means "House of the Sun," and many visitors come Upcountry before dawn to catch the sunrise, and then stay to hike or camp.

WHAT TO SEE

★HALEAKALA NATIONAL PARK (1) *(travel from Kahului via Hwy. 37 to 377 to 378, no public transportation available, 808-572-4400, www.nps.gov/hale, open 24 hours)* is the home of Haleakala, the largest dormant volcano on Earth, rising 10,023 feet into the sky. Legend has it the summit provided a convenient stepstool from which mythical demigod Maui lassoed the sun in order to slow its journey across the sky. (Hawaiians wanted a longer day—who you gonna call? Clever Maui is also said to have pulled the Hawaiian Islands out of the sea with a fishhook.) Part of the Hawaii Volcanoes National Park System, the park stretches from the mountain's summit to a 24,000-acre-plus wilderness area to the tropical east coast of the island, Kipahulu *(accessed via the Hana Highway; see Chapter 2)*. Haleakala has erupted several times within the last thousand years, so scientists technically consider it active. Its climate covers a range of natural environments: multihued deserts, scrublands, fern-

filled cloud forests, and coastal waterfalls and pools. It also contains more
endangered species than any other in
the National Park system, among
them the Hawaiian goose, or *nene*
(named for its call: "nay-nay"), and
the *'ahinahina*, or silversword plant, which may bloom
but once in 50 years.

The favorite must-see is catching a **Haleakala Sunrise (2)**
*(park Web site has complete details: www.nps.gov/hale/plan
yourvisit/sunrise-and-sunset.htm).* On a clear morning,
the sun rising over the sea is a mystical (yet often bone-
chilling) experience. Samuel Clemens (Mark Twain)
called it "the sublimest spectacle I ever witnessed." All
the islands of *Maui nui* seem close enough to touch.
Though the summit itself is always clear, the world
below is often immersed in clouds, and you won't see the
sun until it breaches them. Sunsets may be cloud-fogged
as well, but visitors are guaranteed a wealth of diamonds
in the starry skies at night. Depending on your starting
point, it can take up to two hours or more to reach the
summit by auto. No food or gas is sold within the park,
so fill up your tank and bring refreshments. Sun wor-
shippers will want to get here no later than 30 minutes
before the sunrise. According to the National Park
Service, there are a number of good locations from
which one can see the sunrise, including the Kalahaku
overlook, House of the Sun visitor center, or summit
building. The temperature can drop below freezing
before sunrise and it's often wet and windy, so wear your

warmest clothes, even if it means layering every piece of clothing you packed (beach towels make handy scarves). On average, the sun rises about 6:56AM on January 1 and 5:30AM on June 1. The sun sets about 6PM on January 1 and 7PM June 1. *(For more on Haleakala, see "What to Do," below.)*

Nicknamed the "Wedding Cake Church" for its unusual octagonal shape, pretty **Holy Ghost Catholic Church (3)** *(4300 Lower Kula Rd., Wiakoa, look for signs from the Kula Hwy./Hwy. 37, 808-878-1261, http://kulacath. ipower.com, services Sa 5PM & Su 9:30AM, gift shop open weekdays 9AM–1PM & after Mass)* dates to the late 1800s. The historic church was built to serve Portuguese Catholic laborers who originally came to Maui from the Azores and Madeira Islands to work on sugar plantations. Its hand-carved gilded altar and Stations of the Cross were made by a 19th-century Austrian master woodworker. The church still holds services and weddings and is the site of the annual spring Pentecost Holy Ghost Feast. If the timing of your visit is fortuitous, you might just be able to buy some of the congregation's highly prized Portuguese sweetbread.

The gates of **Hui No'eau Visual Arts Center (4)** *(2841 Baldwin Ave., Makawao, 808-572-6560, www.hui noeau.com/about.php, M–F 10AM–4PM)* open onto ten acres of gardens and a C. W. Dickey-designed 1917 plantation mansion built for pineapple baron Harry Baldwin and his wife Ethel. Mrs. Baldwin founded the society in 1934; its resident artists and touring exhibits make it one of the premier art stops on the island. A free one-hour self-guided tour takes visitors through the studios, current exhibits, the manicured grounds, and the center's history. Recent exhibits have featured master kite makers, avant-garde woodcut printmaking, alchemy, and more.

WHAT TO DO
Hiking:

Haleakala National Park (1) *(travel from Kahului via Hwy. 37 to 377 to 378, 808-572-4400, www.nps.gov/hale, open 24 hours, note: no food or gas sold within the park)* offers a variety of hiking trails that make the unique ter-

rain accessible on foot. The three major trails in the park's wilderness area are connected: scenic **Sliding Sands** *(4-mile trail to the crater floor, considered the main trail)* **Halemau'u** *(also to the crater floor)*, and **Kaupo** *(all the way down the mountain & the most strenuous)*. The park also offers ranger-led walks of varying difficulty and informational programs. Stop by its visitor centers to check on current offerings, check the park's Web site *(www.nps.gov/hale)*, or call 808-572-4400. Examples: **Walk on the Wet Side** *(meet at Hosmer Grove, offered about 1 Su per month, call for reservations up to 1 week in advance, 808-572-4459)*, a muddy, wet, and moderately strenuous five-hour, five-mile hike into Nature Conservancy's limited access **Waikamoi Preserve**. **Waikamoi Cloud Forest Hike** *(meet at Hosmer Grove, tours*

70

M & Th 9AM, staff & weather permitting, arrive 15 min. early, call for reservations up to 1 wk in advance, 808-572-4459) takes you into the preserve for an appreciation of native cloud forests, plants, birds, and invertebrates (three miles, three hours). Wear layers and sturdy shoes, bring rain gear and water. The rangers also offer a one-hour nighttime **Kilo Hoku Star Program** *(Hosmer Grove, occasional evenings May–Sept)*, identifying major constellations and revealing secrets of Polynesian navigation. Wear warm clothes and bring a blanket and flashlight.

For those unfamiliar with the territory and difficulty, consider a fun and informative Haleakala introduction with **Hike Maui (5)** *(meet in Kahului, 866-324-MAUI or 808-879-5270, www.hikemaui.com 4- & 8-mile Haleakala hikes available as well as waterfall hikes & other programs)*; its guides are versed in Hawaiian history, culture, geology, and botany. For a touch of the Pacific Northwest on Maui, hike the trails at seldom-used **Polipoli Spring State Recreation Area (6)** *(nearly 10 miles upland from Kula on Waipoli Rd. off Kekaulike Ave./Hwy. 377; 808-984-8109, www.hawaiistateparks.org/parks/maui/index.cfm?park_id=39, daily 6AM–6PM)*, with its unexpected stand of red-  woods and other imported trees planted by the Civilian Conservation Corps as part of a 1930s reforestation program. Note: The road to the area may or may not be paved after a few miles, depending on ongoing paving progress; four-wheel-drive vehicles recommended. The recreation area's **Plum**, **Redwood**, **Haleakala Ridge**, and **Polipoli** trails form a 3-½-mile loop to hike. Note: Park officials suggest you wear bright-colored clothing, as hunters may be in the area. There is one cabin; camping is also permitted *(see page 82).*

More Activities:

Biking down Haleakala is a 30-miles-plus thrill ride, and Maui's many tour operators offer a panoply of choices. Most will pick you up at a specific starting point (some-

times at your hotel) early in the morning (3:30AM, anyone?), get you pumped with coffee during the van ride up the mountain to take in the famous sunrise, then equip you with helmets, wind-

breakers, and bikes with heavy-duty brakes for the ride downhill. Most tours take an entire day. **Maui Downhill (7)** *(199 Dairy Rd., Kahului, 808-871-2155, www.maui downhill.com, hours vary by tour)* offers a variety of catered tours and sunset rides, accompanied by tour van. Those who prefer an unescorted ride down might check out **Haleakala Bike Company (8)** *(Haiku Marketplace, 810 Haiku Rd., Haiku, 808-575-9575, www.bike maui.com, hours vary by tour)*, which leaves riders on their own after a bike comfort check and safety briefing.

Ride horseback through a working cattle ranch, eucalyptus forests, and lush green pastures at family-owned **Pi'iholo Ranch (9)** *(Waiahiwi Rd., Makawao, 808-357-5544, www.piiholo.com, 3 rides per day M–Sa for up to 6* *guests; private rides & lessons available; advance reservations required);* your experience includes a dose of family history and information on natural horsemanship. **Haleakala on Horseback (10)** *(808-871-0990, www. haleakalaonhorseback.com, check-in 8:30AM, reservations required)* is a unique way to cover territory within the volcano's crater itself. Check in at Haleakala's House of the Sun Visitor Center for one of two trail rides—the first is eight miles long; the other, for experienced riders, is 12 miles long. Windbreaker, gloves, and lunch provided. The tour operator's **Kula Kai Farms** *(www. kulakaifarms.com)* also offers youth day camps and lessons in riding and horsemanship. For a guided trail ride on Haleakala's southwest side, try **Makena Stables (11)** *(Ulupalakua Ranch, 808-879-0244, www.makena stables.com, morning & sunset rides by reservation).* The trail starts at Ulupalakua Ranch and offers panoramic views of the southern slope of Haleakala, the lava fields, La Perouse Bay, and the islands of Hawaii, Kaho'olawe, Molokini, Lana'i, and Moloka'i. Your ride might also provide glimpses of axis deer on land or whales and dolphins in the bay.

In Kula, 4,000 feet above sea level, **O'o Farm (12)** *(north side of Waipoli Rd., Kula, 808-667-4341, www.oofarm.com, tours W, Th 10:30AM by reservation)* is the organic, biodynamic farm that supplies star chef James McDonald and celebrated Lahaina restaurants

Pacific'O, I'O, and the Feast at Lele *(see pages 112 & 115)*. An hour-long gourmet tour given by Richard, the farm manager (who doffs a straw hat in the evenings for his role as resident wine expert with owner Stephan) reveals the challenges and rewards of cultivating fresh fruit and vegetables in Kula's fertile volcanic soil. Visitors savor scenic Upcountry views while helping gather fresh ingredients; farm chef Sean uses these and others to prepare an après-tour repast for visitors. Bring a bottle of wine to share.

Just up the road from O'o Farm, **Ali'i Kula Lavender Farm (13)** *(1100 Waipoli Rd., Kula, 808-878-3004, www.aliikulalavender.com, open daily, walking tours offered throughout the day)* offers tours of the farm's lavender plants as well as other exotic flora. Lunch and tea service, workshops, and other events are offered. Among the dozens of products featured in the farm shop, the organic lavender waterless hand soap is a favorite. Enjoy a little local history along with the homegrown products at **Shim Farm (14)** *(625 Middle Rd., Kula, 808-876-0055, www.shimfarmtour.com, tours offered during coffee season Feb.1–July 31, reservations required)*, a small plantation. The original Shim family home is on the property, along with a lava tube, exotic flowers, fruit trees, and a coffee processing operation. The guided tour takes an hour and includes information about coffee, protea, and the history of the Chinese in Kula, along with a walk through the farm. You may buy the results of Mr. Shim's labor right here.

By now you've figured out that Upcountry is Maui's Garden of Eden. For one more place to appreciate some of the most exotic and beautiful plants in the world, take a self-guided tour at **Kula Botanical Gardens (15)** *(638 Kekaulike Ave./junction routes 37 & 377, Kula, 808-878-1715, www.kulabotanicalgarden.com, daily 9AM–4PM)*, featuring *tikis*, a carp pond, Christmas tree farm, an aviary, and waddling *nenes*. **Sunrise Country Market & Protea Farm (16)** *(16157 Haleakala Hwy./Hwy. 378, ¼-mile south of Haleakala National Park sign, market 808-878-1600, farm 808-876-7768, www.sunrise protea.com, daily 7AM–3PM)* offers snacks, picnic tables, and a botanical garden of exotic protea flowers. Proteas may resemble colorful pincushions, feathered cups, or other unusual forms. Originally from South Africa, the flowers thrive in Upcountry Maui. **Enchanting Floral Gardens (17)** *(mile marker 10, east side of Kula Hwy./Hwy. 37, Kula, 808-878-2531, www.flowersofmaui.com, daily 9AM–5PM)* is a private garden that fills eight acres with more than 2,000 exotic plants.

Friendly dairy goats, as well as dogs, cats, and Charlie the potbellied pig invite you to visit prairie-like lower Kula and **Surfing Goat Dairy Farm (18)** *(3651 Oma'opio Rd., Kula, 808-878-2870, www.surfinggoatdairy.com, tours M, W, F 10AM–4PM, Tu, Th, Sa 10AM–3:15PM, Su 10AM–1PM; store hours: M–Sa 10AM–5PM, Su 10AM–2PM, check Web site for other tour options)*. The dairy produces over 25 different cheeses, including many national award winners, and (ready for this?) goat cheese truffles, too! This is one of the most popular farm tours on the island. Take some cheese home with you— "Da feta mo' betta!"

Sample Maui wines in the former King's Cottage, built for Hawaiian royalty, and enjoy the surrounding picnic area at **Tedeschi Vineyards (19)** *(Kula Hwy./Rte. 37, Kula, from central Maui, take Hana Hwy./Hwy. 36 to Haleakala Hwy./Hwy. 37 to Keokea; pass the Henry Fong Store on the right, continue on 5.1 miles to Ulupalakua Ranch. Winery is just past the ranch headquarters & store. 808-878-6058, www.mauiwine.com, daily 9AM–5PM; tours offered at 10:30AM, 1:30PM, & 3PM).* A Ulupalakua Ranch enterprise, the winery's first "vintage" was Maui Blanc Pineapple Wine. Grape wines from mature vines followed in the 1980s. The vineyard now produces a dozen different blends, both still and sparkling, made from grapes and grape-and-tropical fruit combinations.

PLACES TO EAT & DRINK
Where to Eat:

Hali'imaile General Store (20) ($$) *(900 Hali'imaile Rd., Hali'imaile, 808-572-2666, www.haliimailegeneralstore. com, M–F 11AM–2:30PM & daily 5:30–9:30PM)* is one of the most popular restaurants on Maui, thanks to Chef Bev Gannon's creativity and plenty of fresh food sources. In a past life, the historic structure served those who worked the local pineapple fields, but its American-Asian menu has made it a modern-day destination for celebs like Elton John and Jack Nicholson and foodies seeking out the crab pizza appetizer and rack of lamb Hunan style.

Eighty-year-old general store **T. Komoda Store & Bakery (21) ($)** *(3674 Baldwin Ave., Makawao, 808-572-7261, M–Tu & Th–F 7AM–5PM, Sa 7AM–2PM, closed W, Su)* turns out sought-after cream puffs, cookies, long Johns, and butter rolls; they're usually sold out by late morning.

Makawao has two excellent cafés: **Café del Sol (22) ($)** *(Courtyard, 3620 Baldwin Ave., Makawao, 808-572-4877, M–Sa 8AM–3PM)*, perfect for early morning coffee and breakfast, thanks to its shady outdoor space, and **Café O'Lei (23) ($)** *(Courtyard, 3669 Baldwin Ave., Makawao, 808-573-9065, 11AM–4PM)* which serves lunch and dinner; this is one of several locations of this chain on the island. **Down to Earth Natural Foods (24) ($)** *(1169 Makawao Ave., Makawao, 808-572-1488, www.downtoearth.org, daily*

8AM–8PM) a branch of the islands' popular health-food chain, offers baked goods, a salad and hot-entrée bar, packaged foods, and produce. **Polli's Mexican Restaurant (25) ($)** *(1202 Makawao Ave., Makawao 808-572-7808, daily 11AM–10PM)* serves much more than Mexican. Its crowd-pleasing menu includes everything from enchiladas to barbecued ribs, and the kitchen offers to make any dish vegetarian on request.

Kula Lodge and Restaurant (26) ($-$$)*(15200 Haleakala Hwy./Hwy. 377, Kula, 808-878-1535, www.kulalodge. com, daily 7AM–10PM)* was built as a rustic private residence in the 1940s, then morphed into a 150-seat restaurant with a garden terrace offering spectacular views. The lodge offers breakfast, lunch, dinner, and the only full-service bar in Kula. Gift shop on site *(see page 80)*. Five rustic chalets are available for overnight stays *(see page 81)*.

Ulupalakua Ranch Deli and Grill (27) ($) *(take Haleakala Hwy./Hwy. 37; at Keokea, stay to the right & continue 5.2 miles to 'Ulupalakua, Kula, 808-878-2561, www. ulupalakuaranch.com, daily 9:30AM–5PM)* serves sandwiches, salads, cheeses, and sweet treats, including 30 kinds of ice cream bars. This is also the place to purchase Maui Cattle Company beef, raised at the ranch without growth stimulants or antibiotics. Get it grilled right here from 11AM–2:30PM. You can also order

'Ulupalakua beef burgers, chicken teriyaki, or kalua pig or elk sandwiches to enjoy at a picnic table on the store's veranda.

Bars & Nightlife:

Makawao may be an unexpected place to find great Italian and one of Maui's best nightclubs, but **Casanova Italian Restaurant & Deli (28) ($-$$)** *(1188 Makawao Ave., intersection Baldwin & Makawao Aves., Makawao, 808-572-0220, www.casanovamaui.com, deli open daily 7:30AM–6PM, restaurant serves lunch M–Sa 11:30AM–2PM, dinner daily 5:30PM–9:30PM, entertainment W, F, Sa to 1AM)* fills the bill and then some for cappuccinos, gourmet pasta, and after-dark action Upcountry. Ladies, don't miss "Wild Wahine Wednesdays," voted "Best Late Night in Maui" and "Best Singles Scene."

WHERE TO SHOP

Makawao is known for its boutiques and art galleries; several are within strolling distance on Baldwin Avenue. Hot Island Glass (29) *(3620 Baldwin Ave.,*

Makawao, 808-572-4527, www.hotislandglass.com, daily 9AM–5PM), a glassworks studio and gallery, produces marvelous works of art. Colorful Aloha Cowboy (30) *(3643 Baldwin Ave., Makawao, 808-573-8190, M–Sa 10AM–6PM)* outfits *paniolos* with authentic and one-of-a-kind Western wear, boots, décor, and tack.

Kula Marketplace (31) *(15200 Haleakala Hwy./Hwy. 377, Kula, 808-878-2135, www.kulamarketplace.com, daily 7AM–7PM)* at **Kula Lodge and Restaurant (27)** *(see also pages 78 & 81)* sells a variety of regional products and arts and crafts, from jams and chocolates to quilts, sculpture, and photography.

Ulupalakua Ranch Store (32) *(end of Kula Hwy./ Rte.37/Thompson Rd./Rte. 31, 'Ulupalakua, 808-878-1202, www.ulupalakuaranch.com, daily 9:30AM–5PM)* carries cowboy hats, bandanas, and belt buckles sporting the ranch logo, local gourmet gifts, and works by local artists. The staff will play samples from the store's array of Hawaiian music CDs at your request.

WHERE TO STAY

Hale Ho'okipa Inn (33) ($$) *(32 Pakani Pl., Makawao, 808-572-6698, www.maui-bed-and-breakfast.com)* is a modernized 1924 plantation home on a quiet, dead-end street less than a mile from the heart of Makawao. The décor is a casual mix of antiques and well-appreciated furnishings. The inn offers three guest rooms and one two-bedroom suite, all with private baths. The suite has access to the kitchen. Continental breakfast may include island coffee blends, teas, and juices; organic fruits; yogurt; bagels or breads; and island jams, jellies, or fruit butters. Enjoy yours under the stately Cook Island pine tree.

Get away from it all at secluded **Olinda Country Cottages and Inn (34) ($$)** *(2660 Olinda Rd., Makawao, 800-932-3435, http://supak.com/olindacountry)*. You'll take the road from Makawao, passing farms, pastures, and cool stands of trees until you're 4,000 feet above the sea. Here, a former protea farm has been re-imagined into a lovely hideaway. The B&B-style inn offers two bedrooms with separate entrances and private baths, two cottages, and a private "Pineapple Sweet."

Kula Lodge and Restaurant (26) *(15200 Haleakala Hwy./Hwy. 377, Kula, 808-878-1535, 800-233-1535, www.kulalodge.com)* *(see also page 78)* has five simple, rustic chalets **($-$$)** that offer amazing views ranging from the island's north shore, across Lana'i and the West Maui Mountains,  to Kaho'olawe and Molokini in the south.

Overnight **camping** is an option at Haleakala National Park (1) *(from Kahului, take Hwy. 37 to 377 to 378, 808-572-4400, www.nps.gov/hale)*. **Hosmer Grove** offers drive-up tent camping for free *(3-night maximum)*. No permit or reservation is required. Tent sites are assigned on a first come, first served basis. Picnic tables, grill, water, and pit toilets provided. The other areas, **Holua**, **Kapalaoa**, and **Paliku**, in the  crater, can only be reached by foot or on horseback. Tent camping is permitted at Holua and Paliku, and each of the areas has a cabin for up to 12 people. Cabins have wood-burning stoves but no electricity; bring warm clothes and bedding. Pit toilets and water are available nearby, but water must be filtered or treated before drinking. Cabins are booked via a monthly lottery; there is a fee and requests must be received over two months in advance of your visit. Tent campsites here are assigned on a first come, first served basis; stop by the park's Headquarters Visitor Center 8AM–3PM. Tent camping is free but requires a permit and a brief orientation. Cabins and tent site stays are limited *(visit www.nps.gov/hale for full details)*.

Located within the fog belt of the Kula Forest Reserve at 6,200 feet, **Polipoli Spring State Recreation Area (6)** *(9.7 miles upland from Kula on Waipoli Rd. off Kekaulike Ave/Hwy. 377; 4-wheel drive recommended; for camping reservation/permit information & applications, call 808-587-0300 8AM–3:30PM M–F Hawaii time or visit* *www.hawaiistateparks.org)* offers tent campsites and one cabin that can accommodate up to ten people. Restrooms are on-site, but you must bring your own water. Notes: Wear bright colors; there may be hunters in the area. And bundle up—nights can be cold at this elevation all year round, and winter temps are frequently below freezing.

I went to Maui to stay a week and remained five.

Mark Twain

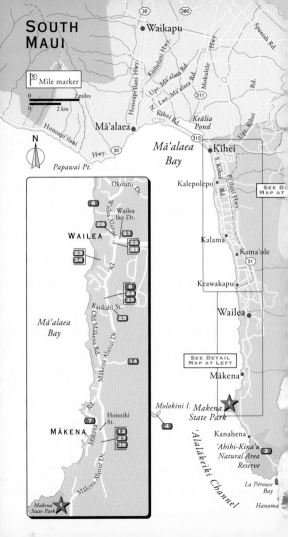

SOUTH MAUI

5 Mile marker

0   2 miles
0   2 km

N

Waikapu

Honoapiʻilani Hwy.
Kūʻīhelani Hwy.
Upr. Māʻalaea Rd.
Lwr. Māʻalaea Rd.
Mokulele
Spanish Rd.
N. Kīhei Rd.
Keālia Pond

Māʻalaea

Papawai Pt.

Honoapiʻilani Hwy.

Māʻalaea Bay

Kīhei

Kalepolepo

S. Kīhei Rd.

Kalama

Piʻilani Hwy.

Upr. Kīhei

Kamaʻole

Keawakapu

Wailea

Mākena

SEE DETAIL MAP AT RIGHT

SEE DETAIL MAP AT LEFT

Makena State Park

Kanahena

ʻAhihi-Kinaʻu Natural Area Reserve

La Pérouse Bay

Hanaka

ʻAlalākeiki Channel

Molokini I.

Okolani Dr.

Wailea Alanui

6

Wailea Ike Dr.

26   21

22   31

WAILEA

23
34

8
24   35

Kaukahi St.

25

Old Mākena Rd.

Mākena Alanui Dr.

14

7

Honoiki St.

MĀKENA

12
27   36

4

Mākena Alanui Dr.

Mākena Rd.

Makena State Park

Māʻalaea Bay

chapter 4

SOUTH MAUI

SOUTH MAUI

What to See:
1. MAKENA STATE PARK ★
2. 'Ahihi-Kina'u Natural Area Reserve
3. La Perouse Bay
4. Molokini

What to Do:
5. Kama'ole 1, Kama'ole 2, Kama'ole 3
6. Ulua Beach
7. Maui Eco Tours
8. Hawaiian Sailing Canoe Adventures
9. Snorkel Bob's
10. Maui Dive Shop
11. Blue Water Rafting
12. Makena Boat Partners
13. Maui Golf Shop
14. Wailea Golf Club

Places to Eat & Drink:
15. Shangri-La by the Sea
16. Stella Blues Caffe
17. Kihei Caffé
18. Koiso Sushi Bar
19. Da Kitchen Express
20. Sarento's On the Beach
21. Joe's Simply Delicious Food
22. Cheeseburger Island Style
23. Humuhumunukunukuapua'a
24. Nick's Fishmarket
25. Mulligan's on the Blue
26. Honua'ula Luau
27. Sunset Lu'au

Where to Shop:
28. Azeka Makai/Azeka Mauka
29. Maui Clothing Outlet
30. Kihei Kalama Village
31. The Shòps at Wailea
32. Farmers' Market of Maui-Kihei
33. Foodland

Where to Stay:
34. Grand Wailea Resort
35. Fairmont Kea Lani Maui
36. Maui Prince Hotel
37. Maui Suncoast Realty
38. AA Oceanfront Condo Rentals
39. Nona Lani Cottages
40. Kai's B&B
41. What a Wonderful World Bed & Breakfast

★ *Top Picks*

SOUTH MAUI

● SNAPSHOT ●

The first thing you notice driving down South Maui's Kihei Road are its hundreds and hundreds of rental condominiums. As you proceed into Wailea and Makena, condos become interspersed with posh hotels. Despite the development, the attractions that launched the building boom are still here and still free: year-round sunshine and incredible beaches. For recreation, South Maui's beaches are arguably among the best on an island known for its world-class sunning and surfing spots.

Kihei is a community of real people who live and work in the area between Kihei Road and the Pi'ilani Highway, or Highway 31, and the locals provide plenty of homey touches that warm up the town: inexpensive eateries of all types, shopping centers with items you can really use, grocery stores, and a community spirit that celebrates ethnic holidays with vigor. Kihei town fronts a series of grassy parks opening onto attractive sand

 beaches and the blue Pacific. First-time and budget-minded visitors can find inexpensive rental condos, reasonably priced food, and plenty to do. It's a good base for island explorations, and an ideal place to take in a spectacular sunset at the end of a busy day.

Wailea is lined with elegant hotels that pamper well-heeled guests with luxe amenities and star-chef restaurants. Golfers won't feel left out, either; some of the most scenic and challenging courses in the country are found here. South of Wailea, Makena State Park is in a class by itself with a bevy of popular beaches. At the end of the road, rocky La Perouse Bay marks the otherworldly site of Maui's last lava flow.

WHAT TO SEE

★**MAKENA STATE PARK (1)** *(Makena Rd., Makena, 808-587-0300, www.hawaiistate parks.org/parks/maui/makena.cfm, daily 6AM–6PM)*, with its 360-foot cinder cone **Pu'u Ola'i** ("Earthquake Hill" or "Red Hill") has two of the best beaches on the island for swimming, bodysurfing, and snorkeling (as always, be aware of changing wind and water conditions). The park (its name *Makena* means "abundance") is also a favorite for enjoying Technicolor sunsets. A Makena Road sign directs visitors to the park access road and a parking lot from which you may access **Makena/Malu'aka Beach**, across from the **Maui Prince Hotel (36)**. Amenities include picnic tables, shade, showers, and restrooms. The second beach is down the road a few hundred yards. You'll know when you see the cars parked along the roadside. **Oneloa Beach** or **"Big Beach"** is a short walk through the trees. Though there are few amenities and not a lot of shade, its inviting golden sands span over two-

TOP PICK!

87

thirds of a mile (*Oneloa* means "long sands"). A trail at the foot of the **Puʻu Olaʻi** cinder cone to the north separates Big Beach from secluded **"Little Beach,"** a favorite of nude bathers. Note: Locals frown upon this activity and it is technically against the law.

Most of **ʻAhihi-Kinaʻu Natural Area Reserve (2)** *(S. Makena Alanui Rd., Keoneʻoʻio, http://hawaii.gov/dlnr/ dofaw/nars/reserves/maui/ahihikinau, accessible areas open 5:30AM–7:30PM)* has been closed by the Board of Land and Natural Resources because of visitor damage to its coral reefs and archaeological sites. You may still snorkel  and swim at ʻAhihi Bay's **Kanahena Cove** (also known as the "Dumps"). Notes: This is a reserve, not a recreational park; there are no amenities. Bring your own drinking water. Beware changing winds and weather and turbulent water. Do not apply sunscreen less than 30 minutes before going in the water; its residue sickens coral. Do not stand on coral. Touching sea turtles or other creatures transmits disease. No fishing or motorized boats permitted. Also part of the reserve, remote **La Perouse Bay (3)** *(end of S. Makena Alanui Rd., accessible areas open 5:30AM– 7:30PM)*, at the site of the last lava flow on Maui, is named for French Admiral Jean-François de Galaup, Comte de La Pérouse, the first European to land on the island in 1786 (a marker here commemorates the event). Hiking is permitted east of the dirt parking area. Wear sturdy shoes—the sharp, hardened *ʻaʻa* lava flows (meaning "stony with rough lava") can slice through flimsy footwear. Do not disturb the archaeological sites in this area.

The crescent-shaped island of **Molokini (4)** *(2-½ miles from Maui, bet. Maui & Kahoʻolawe Island)* is a partially submerged volcanic crater.

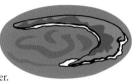

It's still considered a spectacular place to snorkel, even though the numbers of boats now visiting the uninhabited 23-acre site (a bird and marine life sanctuary) have caused fish to flee to feeding areas with fewer masked humans. If you go, go early in the morning.

WHAT TO DO
Beaches:
South Maui boasts terrific beaches, from the **Makena State Park (1)** beaches mentioned above *(see page 87)* to the popular trio of Kamaʻole Beach Parks: **Kamaʻole 1, Kamaʻole 2,** and **Kamaʻole 3 (5)** *(S. Kihei Rd., Kihei, 808-879-4364, 7AM–7PM)*. Easily accessible on foot from main drag South Kihei Road, the beaches have lifeguards *(8AM–4:30PM)*, shade, restrooms, outdoor showers, and picnic tables. A personal favorite for easy snorkeling access and amenities such as showers, **Ulua Beach (6)** *(off Wailea Alanui Rd., Wailea, 7AM–7PM)* is at the end of the turnoff just before the **Shops at Wailea (31)** (look for the sign that says "Beach Access"). The parking lot only has a few spaces, so get there early to observe the bounty of tropical fish off the rocks west of the beach.

Watersports:

Maui Eco Tours (7)  *(departs from Makena Landing, S. Makena Rd., Makena, 808-891-2223, www.mauiecotours.com, tour hours vary)* offers small group, kayak-and-snorkel tours aimed at acquainting visitors with sea life. Guides snorkel with you, and the tour company has programs for families and for experienced kayakers. **Hawaiian Sailing Canoe Adventures (8)**

(departs from Fairmont Kea Lani Hotel, 4100 Wailea Alanui, Kihei, 808-281-9301, www.mauisailingcanoe.com, tours leave daily 8AM & 10AM from Polo Beach) 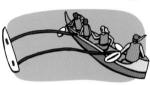 allow you to be part of the paddling crew aboard the traditional outrigger sailing canoe *Hina* (named after Hawaii's moon goddess). Or you can just relax, snorkel, and learn about Hawaiian history, culture, and ancient navigation.

For a private, out-of-the-ordinary tour, join acclaimed marine biologist/guide Ann Fielding's **Snorkel Maui** *(locations vary, 808-572-8437, http://users.maui.net/~annf, about 7:30AM–12:30PM)*. Participants (kids ages 7–up & beginners are welcome) receive instruction on the provided equipment, a pre-snorkel talk on Hawaii's unique marine life, plus further instruction when in the water, snacks, and a review.

If you'd prefer to just rent the equipment and go out on your own, try the North Kihei branch of **Snorkel Bob's (9)** *(Azeka II Shopping Center, 1279 S. Kihei Rd., #310, Kihei, 808-875-6188, www.snorkelbob.com, daily 8AM–5PM)*. Or try its South Kihei branch *(Kamaole Beach Center, 2411 S. Kihei Rd., Kihei, 808-879-7449, daily 8AM–5PM)* or **Maui Dive Shop (10)** *(Kihei Outlet Center, 1455 S. Kihei Rd., 808-879-3388 or 800-542-3483, www.mauidiveshop.com, daily 6AM–9PM)*.

Riding a raft is much like being aboard a bucking bronco—only the experience lasts a bit longer! **Blue Water Rafting (11)** *(departs from Kihei boat ramp just south of Kamaole Beach Park III, 808-879-7238, www.bluewaterrafting.com, hours vary)* was one of the first to offer the wild ride kids (of all ages) love. Hold on tight and prepare to get bumped and soaked during its tours to Kanaio and Molokini. **Makena Boat Partners (12)** *(departs from Maui Prince Hotel, 5400 Makena Alanui Dr., Makena, 808-879-7218, www.kaikanani.com, excursion hours vary)* offers a jolt-free early-morning "Molokini Express" trip aboard 64-foot catamaran *Kai Kanani*. Continental breakfast, gear, and instruction provided. They feature other boat adventures, too.

Golf:

Maui Golf Shop (13) *(357 Huku Li'i Pl., Kihei, 808-875-4653 or 800-981-5512, www.mauigolfshop.com or www.golf-maui.com, call for hours)* rents clubs at reasonable rates, provides course bookings and advice about Maui golf courses, and offers online discounts. The

Gold, Emerald, and Blue courses of 54-hole **Wailea Golf Club (14)** *(100 Golf Club Dr. off Wailea Alanui Rd., Wailea, 808-875-7450, www.waileagolf.com)* are top shelf all the way. The Gold Course is the most demanding and consistently rated as one of Hawaii's best.

PLACES TO EAT & DRINK
Where to Eat:
Some of the island's best Indian cuisine can be found at **Shangri-La by the Sea (15) ($-$$)** *(Menehune Shores Resort, 760 S. Kihei Rd., Ste. 109, Kihei, 808-875-4555, www.shangri-labythesea.com, daily 11AM–2:30PM, 5–10PM)*. There are plenty of chicken and lamb dishes, and an extensive vegetarian menu. **Stella Blues Café (16) ($)** *(Azeka II Shopping Center, 1279 S. Kihei Rd., #201, Kihei, 808-874-3779, www.stellablues.com, daily 7:30AM–11PM)* is a find for good, inexpensive American food. The "build-your-own omelets" are a breakfast favorite. Other crowd-pleasers include "Mama Tried" meat loaf with mashed potatoes and vegetables. Several Italian specialties star in the lunch and dinner menus. Fancy, it ain't, but **Kihei Caffé (17) ($)** *(1945 S. Kihei Rd., Kihei, 808-879-2230, daily 5AM–2PM)* serves one of the best breakfasts this side of heaven. Some swear by the

banana-macadamia pancakes with coconut syrup. Homemade burgers are made from local beef. Come in your swimsuit and join the surfers on the patio. The owner's mom, Miss Bunny, may come by to check on your food and offer travel tips.

Koiso Sushi Bar (18) ($-$$) *(2395 S. Kihei Rd., Ste. 113, Kihei, 808-875-8258, daily 5:30PM–9:30PM)* is tiny, has a limited menu, and is unpretentious at best. The tip-off is the number of Japanese tourists

seated at the tables. Koiso serves the freshest fish—"pure sushi bliss," according to one fan—and the owners couldn't be nicer. Fill up without emptying the wallet at **Da Kitchen Express (19) ($)** *(Rainbow Mall, 2439 S. Kihei Rd., Kihei, 808-875-7782, www.da-kitchen.com, daily 9AM–9PM)*, serving up eat-in or take-out breakfast omelets, sandwiches, salads, Hawaiian-style plate lunches, and "oodles of noodles." Fabulous views, fine wine, handcrafted pastas, and seafood with a Mediterranean twist attract diners to romantic **Sarento's On the Beach (20) ($$)** *(2980 S. Kihei Rd., Kihei, 808-875-7555, www.tristarrestaurants.com/sarentos_maui, 5:30PM–10PM, lounge open 5PM–midnight).*

When a former showbiz whiz joins forces with an award-winning chef, the result is **Joe's Simply Delicious Food (21) ($-$$)** *(131 Wailea Ike Pl., above Wailea Tennis Center, Wailea, 808-875-7767, www.bevgannon restaurants.com/joes, daily 5:30PM–9PM)*. Joe and Bev Gannon of Upcountry's Hali'imaile General Store fame, *(see page 77)* create "down-home" crowd-pleasers like slow-roasted prime rib with whipped potatoes, meat loaf with Texas barbecue sauce, and grilled pork chops with homemade applesauce and warm potato salad in bacon vinaigrette. Plenty of fresh fish, too, all served in pleasant surrounds. Popular **Cheeseburger Island Style (22) ($)** *(Shops at Wailea, 3750 Wailea Alanui Dr., Wailea, 808-874-8990, www.cheeseburgerland.com, daily 8AM–10PM)* serves breakfast, lunch, and dinner at reasonable prices.

With a tongue-twister of a name, **Humuhumunukunukuapua'a (23) ($$$)** *(Grand Wailea Resort, 3850 Wailea Alanui Dr., Wailea, 808-875-1234, www.grandwailea.com/dining/humu.aspx, dinner 5:30PM–9PM; bar opens 5PM)* (pronounced "humu humu nuku nuku a pu aa"—it's the name of Hawaii's colorful state fish), is a foodie's dream. The setting couldn't be more of a dining delight: open to the warmth of the evening sun, the thatched-roof restaurant floats on a sparkling lagoon shimmering with koi. Fresh seafood is elegantly presented and served. Another big-hotel restaurant standout: **Nick's Fishmarket (24) ($$-$$$)** *(Fairmont Kea Lani Maui, 4100 Wailea Alanui, Wailea, 808-879-7224, www.tristarrestaurants.com/nicks, dinner 5:30PM–10PM, lounge opens 5PM)*, featuring top quality ingredients, expert preparation, and gorgeous surrounds. Dine *al fresco* under a trellis laden with fragrant stephanotis flowers and sparkling lights.

Bars, Nightlife, & Lu'aus:

The intrepid Irishmen at **Mulligan's on the Blue (25) ($$)** *(on the Wailea Blue Golf Course, Wailea Golf Club, across from the Kea Lani Hotel, 100 Kaukahi St., Wailea, 808-874-1131, www.mulligansontheblue.com, daily*

8AM–1AM) offer hearty pub food, beers on tap, satellite sports, and live entertainment most nights, from Gypsy jazz musicians to Celtic crooners to "talk-story" blues/jazz/rock guitarist Willie K.

Eat light before a *lu'au*. The **Honua'ula Luau (26) ($$$$)** *(Wailea Marriott Resort, 3700 Wailea Alanui Rd., Wailea, call for reservations, 808-875-7710 or 808-879-1922, www.marriott.com/hotels/travel/hnmmc-wailea-beach, M, Th, F, Sa check-in 5PM)* is a theatrical feast that highlights Maui's heritage, with sunset torch lighting, hula dancing, chants, photo ops, and more. Expect an overwhelming buffet of Hawaiian food and drink. The **Sunset Lu'au (27) ($$$$)** *(Maui Prince Hotel, 5400 Makena Alanui Rd., Makena, reservations: 808-877-HULA or 4852, www.princeresortshawaii.com/maui-luau.php, Tu–Th 5PM–8:30PM)* is widely considered one of Maui's best. It includes roasted *kalua* pig from a steaming *imu* (pit barbecue), an all-you-can-eat buffet with *poi* and *lomi* salmon, and lavish Polynesian entertainment—hula, Tahitian, and Maori dancing with a big fire-dance finish.

WHERE TO SHOP

Kihei is mall central; you'll find as many here as in Kahului. Sister shopping centers Azeka Makai and Azeka Mauka (28) *(1279 & 1280 S. Kihei Rd., corner of Pi'ikea Ave., Kihei, 808-879-5000, http://mwgroup.com/azeka. asp)* straddle the road in central Kihei (*makai* means "toward the sea," *mauka* means "away from the sea/toward the mountain"). They share more than 50 shops and eateries, as well as the post office and banks. Local events, such as the mid-August Japanese *obon* festival, are sometimes held here. *Obon* celebrates the lives of those who have passed on; it's similar to Mexico's Day of the Dead. Maui Clothing Outlet (29) *(Kihei Gateway Center, 362 Huku Li'i Pl., #106, Kihei, 808-875-0308, www.mauiclothingcompany.com, M–Sa 10AM–7PM, Su 10AM–5PM)* is a favorite place to shop; it offers a variety of quality men's and women's Hawaiian-style clothing at discount prices. Come here if you're looking for something besides the sarongs you see everywhere else. Lively Kihei Kalama Village (30) *(1941 S. Kihei Rd., Kihei, 808-879-6610, daily 9AM–7PM, open-air marketplace shops open 10AM–7:30PM)* is a maze of independent sellers hawking everything from jewelry and fine art to trinkets, T-shirts, and Crocs. Eateries here run the gamut of international cuisines.

South Maui's premier shopping center, The Shops at Wailea (31) *(3750 Wailea Alanui Rd., Wailea, 808-891-6770, www.shopsatwailea.com)* includes Tiffany & Co., Louis Vuitton, Gucci, Fendi, Banana Republic, and ABC Stores, a local chain that stocks fun Hawaiian sundries.

For fresh fruits, veggies, juices, cheeses, and coffee, stop by the Farmers' Market of Maui-Kihei (32) *(61 S. Kihei Rd.*

across from Kihei Canoe Club, 808-875-0949, M–Th 8AM–4PM, F 8AM–5PM). You'll also find baked goods, salsas, and fresh flowers. Local supermarket mainstay Foodland (33) *(1881 S. Kihei Rd., #1, Kihei, 808-879-9350, open 24 hrs)* is a good place to pick up deli specials like *huli huli* roasted chicken and *lomi lomi* salmon, as well as grocery items and beer, wine, and spirits.

WHERE TO STAY

Grand Wailea Resort (34) ($$$) *(3850 Wailea Alanui Dr., Wailea, 808-875-1234 or 800-888-6100, www.grandwailea.com)* is everything you'd expect an ultra-luxury hotel to be: fine art everywhere (they give

tours); a pool mosaic depicting a hibiscus flower; a series of nine multi-level pools linked by a river with waterslides, waterfalls, even a water elevator. Restaurants, bars, and Spa Grande (a "Top Ten"–rated spa) make this a fabulous getaway. Set on 22 acres of landscaped perfection, the Fairmont Kea Lani Maui (35) ($$$) *(4100 Wailea Alanui Rd., Wailea, 808-875-4100 www.fairmont.com/kealani)* is the only luxury all-suite and villa oceanfront resort in the islands. Suites offer private *lanais*, marble bathrooms, wet bars, microwaves, coffeemakers, and compact refrigerators. Two-story oceanfront villas include three-bedroom retreats with courtyards, plunge pools, kitchens, extra baths, and washers/dryers. Guests enjoy recreational and cultural activities. Want to relax away from it all? Maui Prince Hotel (36) ($$$) *(5400 Makena Alanui Dr., Makena, 808-874-1111, www.*

princeresortshawaii.com/maui-prince-hotel.php) will take you there. Built around an Asian meditation garden with stone paths, waterfalls, and streams filled with shimmering koi fish, this *Travel & Leisure* magazine "Top 25" Hawaii hotel boasts over 300 guest rooms, including 19 luxury suites, two Robert Trent Jones Jr.—designed golf courses, tennis courts, spa service, restaurants, lounges, and a white sand beach. The *keiki* club allows young guests to go fishing, build sandcastles, and learn hula dancing, among other activities.

Condo rentals are a mainstay in South Maui. Some companies handle only one condo, others have units all over; some charge booking fees, and almost all charge cleaning fees in addition to the rental cost. Ask for what you want (quiet location, updated amenities, an elevator, easy parking, or washer/dryer). Almost all the condos in Kihei are within walking distance to the beach. **Maui Suncoast Realty (37) ($-$$$$)** *(380 Huku Li'i Pl., #104, Kihei, 808-874-1048 or 800-800-8608, www.mauisun coast.com)* handles condos, homes, and cottage properties. They work to match your needs and don't charge a booking fee. One of their options: inexpensive **Maui Vista ($)**, one-bedroom units with amenities across from

Kamaole 1 (5) beach *(see page 89)*. **AA Oceanfront Condo Rentals (38) ($-$$$$)** *(1279 S. Kihei Rd., Ste. 107, Kihei, 808-879-7288 or 800-488-6004, www.aaoceanfront.com)* manages properties from

north Kihei to Wailea in all price ranges. Preview properties on its Web site.

Nona Lani Cottages (39) ($-$$) *(455 S. Kihei Rd., Kihei, 800-733-2688 or 808-879-2497, www.nonalanicottages.com, minimum stay 4–7 nights)* is right across the street from scenic Sugar Beach, a windsurfing favorite. Eight cottages (four oceanfront, four garden) are located on two acres of landscaped grounds. Each cottage features a carpeted living area with a sofa/day bed, a bedroom with queen bed, TV, ceiling fan (no air conditioning), and a kitchen. Craving extra quiet? Ask for a garden cottage away from the street.

The neighborhood surrounding **Kai's B&B (40) ($)** *(80 E. Welakahao Rd., Kihei, 800-905-8424 ext. 24 or 808-874-6431, www.mauibb.com)* can be a bit unsightly, but the B&B itself is surrounded by a wall, making it very private. It's two blocks from the beach, and features two bedrooms, a studio with kitchen, and a two-bedroom cottage set back from the main house. The owners place a breakfast basket outside each guest room daily, and provide bicycles, beach equipment, and hot tub and washer/dryer use. Budget-minded travelers may find this a good value. **What a Wonderful World Bed & Breakfast (41) ($-$$)** *(2828 Umalu Pl., Kihei, 800-943-5804, http://amauibedandbreakfast.com)* is a lovely home in a quiet residential neighborhood away from the beach and the main streets. Four spacious suites feature private baths, and guests wake up to a Continental breakfast. Beach chairs and towels are provided.

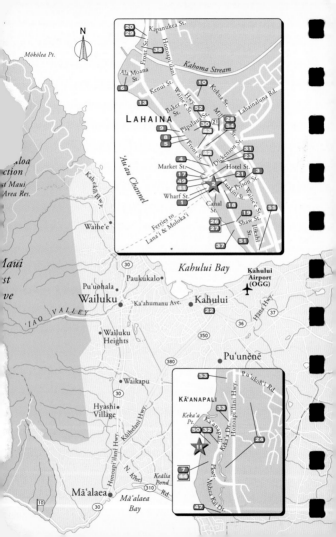

chapter 5

WEST MAUI

WEST MAUI

What to See:

1. Lahaina Visitor Center
2. BANYAN TREE ★
3. Hale Pa'ahao
4. Baldwin Home
5. Wo Hing Temple
6. Lahaina Jodo Mission
7. Whalers Village Museum
8. *Ulalena*
9. Warren and Annabelle's
10. Sugar Cane Train

What to Do:

11. KA'ANAPALI BEACH ★
12. Mile Marker 14 Beach
13. Pu'unoa "Baby Beach"
14. Honokowai Beach Park
15. Napili Beach
16. Honolua Bay
17. *Trilogy*
18. Pacific Whale Foundation
19. Nancy Emerson School of Surfing
20. West Maui Sport
21. Atlantis Attractions
22. Hike Maui
23. Maui Eco-Adventures
24. Ka'anapali Golf Resort

Places to Eat & Drink:

25. Chez Paul
26. Pacific'O
27. I'O
28. Gerard's Restaurant
29. Aloha Mixed Plate
30. Cilantro Grill
31. Penne Pasta
32. Tiki Terrace
33. CJ's Deli & Diner
34. Honokowai Okazuya & Deli
35. Sea House Restaurant
36. Sansei Seafood Restaurant & Sushi Bar
37. Feast at Lele
38. Old Lahaina Lu'au
39. Maui Brewing Co. Brewpub
40. Masters of Hawaiian Slack Key Guitar

Where to Shop:

41. Banyan Tree Gallery
42. Village Galleries
43. Martin Lawrence Galleries
44. Whalers Village
45. Maui's Own Gift & Craft Fair
46. Honokowai Market

★ *Top Picks*

Where to Stay:

Never turn your back
on the ocean.

Hawaiian saying

● **SNAPSHOT** ●

West Maui buzzes with nightlife, shopping, art, and fine dining. The former Hawaiian capital and old whaling port of Lahaina (once known as *Lele*, "relentless sun") has morphed into a tourist hot spot and nightlife hub. Up the road, the Ka'anapali coast offers a superb beach and fine hotels with restaurants and entertainment. As Honoapi'ilani Highway (Route 30) follows the coastline of the island to the west and north, areas once accessed via two-lane roads have become residential neighborhoods, hotels, condominium complexes, and shopping centers. The villages of Honokowai, Napili, and Kapalua all offer something for visitors, including inexpensive condo rentals, family resorts, and planned communities swathed in luxury. The Kapalua/West Maui airport provides direct service to West Maui. It's possible to spend an entire vacation here with everything one might wish for close by. A series of beaches offers everything from calm waters for toddlers' first swim lessons to big waves for Honolua Bay surfers.

WHAT TO SEE

Lahaina juggles ancient heritage with 21st-century amusements; it has a long history of being a party town. King Kamehameha ruled the Hawaiian Islands from here before

103

moving his court to Honolulu in 1845. Whaling vessels anchored in the local harbor from the 1840s through the 1860s. Herman Melville, author of *Moby-Dick*, was a visitor. As whaling waned, sugar reigned, and became the town's mainstay industry for a century, attracting waves of immigrant workers. Today, the main section of town is filled with art galleries, chic shops, gourmet eateries, and boutiques, rather than bordellos and sea-side dives. Bronze plaques around and about Front Street point out key sites on the self-guided Lahaina Historic Trail *Ala Hele Mo'olelo O Lahaina*. Start with a visit to the Lahaina Visitor Center (1) *(648 Wharf St., Lahaina, 808-667-9193, www.visitlahaina.com, daily 9AM–5PM)*.

TOP PICK!

Lahaina's amazing ★BANYAN TREE (2) *(Banyan Court, Front & Canal Sts., Lahaina, 808-661-4685, www.co.maui.hi.us/parks/maui/west/LahainaBanyan.htm, open daily)* is the

largest in the United States. Brought from India and planted here in 1873, the sprawling, 60-foot tree now covers the town square. Its multiple trunks support limbs just high enough for shade seekers to walk under. The park under the tree is the site of community gatherings and art exhibits. Every second and fourth weekend, **Art in the Park** *(Banyan Court, 808-661-0111, www.lahaina-arts.org)* brings visitors and artists together here to view paintings, limited edition prints, and crafts.

"Stuck-in-Irons House" **Hale Pa'ahao (3)** *(187 Prison St., Lahaina, 808-667-1985, daily 10AM–4PM)* was a jail for Lahaina's rowdy 1850s whalers and sailors, including those caught drinking *'awa* (kava moonshine). Breaking the rules had severe penalties: flogging, solitary confinement, iron shackles, food limitations, head shaving, or—*eek!*—a shower bath. Missionary and Harvard-trained physician Reverend Dwight Baldwin and his family occupied the **Baldwin Home (4)** *(120 Dickenson St., Lahaina, 808-661-3262, daily 10AM–4PM)*, Lahaina's oldest, in the mid-19th century. The two-foot-thick coral-and-rock walls of the two-story structure kept it cool year-round. The home served as dispensary, clinic, and guesthouse—often all at once. It's decorated with furniture and artifacts of the period.

A "Dancing Lion of Taipei," a traditional symbol of good luck, greets visitors as they enter lovely **Wo Hing Temple (5)** *(858 Front St., Lahaina, 808-661-5553, www.lahainarestoration.org, daily 10AM–4PM)*. Built in 1912 by Chinese immigrants who worked in the sugar cane fields, the building was used as a social hall. The Lahaina Restoration Foundation now operates the temple as a museum; it has a sacred altar room on the second floor for religious ceremonies. The tranquil campus of **Lahaina Jodo Mission (6)** *(12 Ala Moana St., Lahaina, 808-661-4304, http://lahainajodomission.org, grounds open*

daily sunrise–sunset) features a graceful Japanese-style Buddhist temple, pagoda, bell tower, and statue of Buddha. Handmade interlocking copper shingles cover the temple's rooftops, and nail-free wood construction exemplifies traditional joinery. A 3,000-pound bell is rung 11 times at 8PM each day; three times to symbolize devotion to Buddha and his teachings, and eight times to represent the eight-fold path (Right Understanding, Purpose, Speech, Conduct, Livelihood, Endeavor, Thought, and Meditation). The 12-foot bronze Buddha statue, one of the largest outside Japan, presides over the grounds.

Whalers Village Museum (7) *(Whalers Village, 2435 Ka'anapali Pkwy., Lahaina, 808-661-5992, www. whalersvillage.com/museum.htm, daily 9AM–10PM)* pres-

ents exhibits on whaling life in the 1800s. A large-scale model of a whaling ship, antique ornaments and utensils, and a collection of scrimshaw (pictures carved on whale teeth and bone) will interest maritime enthusiasts and collectors. The museum's reconstructed ship forecastle illustrates the tight quarters whalers endured during long voyages.

A family-friendly stage show with a historical/mythical theme, *Ulalena (8)* *(878 Front St., 808-661-9913 or 877-688-4800, www.mauitheatre.com)* explores Hawaii's origins and culture. It's filled with colorful, exciting performances by dancers and acrobats, and great music—think Cirque du Soleil with a tropical twist. At Warren and Annabelle's (9) *(900 Front St., Ste. A202, Lahaina, 808-667-MAGIC [6244], www.warrenandannabelles.com, M–Sa 1st show check-in 5PM, 2nd show check-in 7:30PM, ages 21 & over)*, the drinks are big, the food tasty, the patter hilarious, and the sleight-of-hand show sensational. Resident magician Warren Gibson is often accompanied by other top conjurers. The show is preceded by a bar-and-appetizers pre-show featuring Annabelle, an invisible pianist who answers questions by picking out tunes on the piano.

All aboard! Drawn by an authentic steam engine, the historic Sugar Cane Train (10) *(17 Kaka'alaneo Dr., Lahaina, 808-667-6851 or 800-499-2307, www.sugarcanetrain.com, call or check Web site for schedule)* chugs along six miles of track between Lahaina and Ka'anapali, delighting passengers large and small.

WHAT TO DO
Beaches:

Sandy, west-facing ★KA'ANAPALI BEACH (11) *(Ka'anapali, access off Ka'anapali Pkwy. & Nohea Kai Dr., open daily)* is the kind of beach you envision when you think "Hawaiian vacation." The beach fronts most of the area's top resorts and the Whaler's Village (44) shopping center, so this is the place to sunbathe and people watch. A concrete path along

TOP PICK!

the beach makes it perfect for sunset strolling. People actually get in the water here, too! The swimming's great when conditions are calm, and the Black Rock area (which divides the beach) is fantastic for snorkeling. Amenities include lifeguards, restrooms, and showers.

The shallow coral offshore of another beach located near **Mile Marker 14 (12)** *(Honoapi'ilani Hwy./Rte. 30 bet. tunnel & Lahaina)* tempts experienced snorkelers. The water at **Pu'unoa "Baby Beach" (13)** *(off Ala Moana St. behind Lahaina Jodo Mission, Lahaina)* is shallow and protected—great for families and those new to ocean swimming. Stretching from the Sheraton Maui to the Hyatt Regency Maui, lined by a palm-shaded walkway, **Honokowai Beach Park (14)** *(Lower Honoapi'ilani Hwy., Lahaina, 808-661-4685, www.co.maui.hi.us)* has a grassy area, two playgrounds, a "comfort station," picnic areas, and water. The surf is broken into pools by stone barriers, providing protected places for small children to swim. Note: No lifeguard on duty. Clean and clear with good swimming and snorkeling, popular **Napili Beach (15)** *(access through Napili Pl. & Hui Dr. off Lower Honoapiilani Rd.)* is considered the best beach in the island's north. After Route 30 becomes two lanes, there is no direct access to **Honolua Bay (16)** *(bet. mile markers 32 & 33, look for cars parked along the road)*, but a 10-minute walk along a path leads to a beach that can offer good swimming and snorkeling in summer and surfing in winter. Tip: Lock valuables in the trunk or take them along. If you just want to watch the surfers (there are professional surf competitions here in winter), try for a parking spot on the cliff beyond and above the bay.

Watersports:

Want to snorkel in pristine waters away from the crowd? Let the professionals of family-owned *Trilogy* **(17)** *(check-in at Lahaina harbor lighthouse, 808-TRILOGY [874-5649] or 888-225-MAUI, www.sailtrilogy.com, hours vary by tour)* take you. Excursions include an early morning "Discover Lana'i Sunrise Sail" to Hulopo'e Beach aboard one of Trilogy's catamarans. Snorkel in protected Hulopo'e Bay, explore the island with a guide, and enjoy a barbecue before your return to Lahaina harbor. A raft trip add-on allows you to explore the island's coast.

Eco tours conducted by **Pacific Whale Foundation (18)** *(most cruises check in at 612 Front St., Lahaina, 808-667-7447 or 800-498-7726, www.pacificwhale.org, hours vary by tour)* are all about ecology, education, and sustainability. (Vessels are powered by bio-diesel; refreshments are served with biodegradable eating utensils.) The foundation also runs snorkeling, dolphin, star-gazing, historical, and sunset cruises, and it is the go-to organization for winter whale watching.

Professional surfer **Nancy Emerson** has taught world-class surfers, celebrities, and everyone in between at her **School of Surfing (19)** *(505 Front St., Ste. 224B, Lahaina, 808-244-7873, www. mauisurfclinics.com, 2-hr. lessons daily at 9AM, noon, 2:30PM; kids' & other lessons/clinics by reservation)*. The school was one of Hawaii's first (1973) and promises that anyone can learn to surf in one lesson. If you're ready to rip on your own, rent gear from **West Maui Sport (20)** *(1287 Front St., Lahaina, 808-661-6252, www.westmauisports.com, M–Sa 8AM–8PM, Su 8AM–6PM)*. They have everything from body boards and surfboards to surf shoes, beach chairs, and coolers. They also put together private kayak and snorkel tours and fishing charters. Getting wet may not be everyone's cup of tea; for dry briny thrills, try a submarine. **Atlantis Attractions (21)** *(658 Front St., Ste. 175, Lahaina, 800-548-6262 or 808-667-2224, www.atlantisadventures.com, tours daily at 9AM, 10AM, noon, 1PM, 2PM)* allows you to board its Atlantis submarine for a tour 100 feet below the surface past sunken ship *Carthaginian II*.

Hiking:

The guides of **Hike Maui (22)** *(meet at commuter parking lot, corner of Pu'unene Ave. & Kuihelani Hwy./Hwy. 380, Kahului, 808-879-5270 or 866-324-MAUI [6284], www.hikemaui.com, hours vary by tour, also see page 71)*, the island's oldest hiking company, are considered "walking encyclopedias." Their three-hour "Short Waterfalls Adventure" takes visitors to West Maui's wild side. See triple cascading waterfalls, swim in pools, discover a hidden waterfall beneath a banyan tree, then continue up a ridge trail for panoramic Pacific

views. **Maui Eco-Adventures (23)** *(180 Dickenson St., Lahaina, 808-661-7720 or 877-661-7720, www.eco maui.com, hours vary by tour)* hosts four- to six-hour "out-of-the-ordinary" hiking adventures in the West Maui mountains and other island locales.

Golf:

Kaanapali Golf Resort (24) *(2290 Kaanapali Pkwy., Lahaina, 808-661-3691 or 866-454-GOLF, www. kaanapaligolfresort.com or www.kaanapali-golf.com, call for hours)* boasts two top courses: a par-70, 6,400-yard Kaanapali Kai Course and the Robert Trent Jones, Sr.–designed Royal Kaanapali Course, a 6,700-yard par-71 course which has challenged golf greats and novices from around the world.

PLACES TO EAT & DRINK
Where to Eat:

French gem **Chez Paul (25) ($$$)** *(821B Olowalu Rd., Olowalu, Rte. 30, 4 miles south of Lahaina town, 808-661-3843, www.chezpaul.net, daily 6PM–9PM)* serves

Provençal-inspired dishes such as *poisson des isles au champagne* (fresh island fish poached in champagne with leeks and capers) and *canard au cassis* (crispy, slow-roasted duck with black currant sauce). Its popular dessert concoction, the "Maui Antoinette," may cause you to lose your head. Acclaimed sister restaurants **Pacific'O (26) ($$)** *(505 Front St., Lahaina, 808-667-4341, www.pacificomaui. com, daily 11AM–4PM, 5:30PM–10PM)* and **I'O ($$) (27)** *(also at 505 Front St., Lahaina, 808-661-8422, serving dinner daily)*, both on the beach, feature the talents of "Maui's Best Chef" *(Maui News)*, James MacDonald, and his almost-too-pretty-to-eat dishes. Great wine selection, too. Award-winning chef Gerard Reversade presides over the four-star French-Hawaiian menu at Maui gem **Gerard's Restaurant (28) ($$-$$$)** *(Plantation Inn, 174 Lahainaluna Rd., Lahaina, 808-661-8939, www.gerardsmaui.com, daily 6PM–9PM)*, considered among America's finest restaurants. Garden patio and veranda seating available.

"Paper plate meets million-dollar view" *(New York Times)* at **Aloha Mixed Plate (29) ($)** *(1285 Front St., Lahaina, 808-661-3322, www.alohamixedplate.com,* *daily 10:30AM–10PM, happy hour 2PM–6PM)*, serving value-priced traditional plate lunches plus foods from Hawaii's ethnic mix, such as teriyaki beef and Thai-style chow mein. **Cilantro Grill (30) ($)** *(170 Papalaua Ave., Old Lahaina Shopping Center, Lahaina, 808-667-5444, www.cilantrogrill.com, M–Th 11AM–9PM, F–Sa 11AM–9PM, Su 11AM–8PM)* offers a bounty of fresh, Mexican-style dishes under $15. Favorites include adobo pork burrito and spicy jicama slaw. For Southern Italian that won't break the bank, **Penne Pasta (31) ($)** *(180 Dickenson St., Lahaina, 808-661-6633, www. pennepastacafe.com, M–F 11AM–9:30PM, Sa–Su 5PM–9:30PM)* invites visitors to take a seat *al fresco* and enjoy baked penne New York, or penne pomodoro, or other pasta dishes. The menu also offers pizza, salads, Italian sandwiches, and desserts (chocolate pot de crème, anyone?).

Larger area hotels have good restaurants, like the **Tiki Terrace (32) ($$–$$$)** *(Ka'anapali Beach Hotel, 2525 Ka'anapali Pkwy., Lahaina, 808-661-0011, www.kbhmaui.com/dining/hotel. html, serving breakfast & dinner daily)*, keeping it Hawaiian with open-air dining and regional cuisine. Kids five and under eat free. **CJ'S Deli & Diner (33) ($)** *(Fairway Shops, 2580 Kekaa Dr., #120, Lahaina, 808-667-0968, www.cjsmaui.com, daily 7AM–8PM)* serves breakfasts, plate lunches, sandwiches, and much more. Comfort food entrées include pot roast, meat loaf, and lasagna. They also have carry-out box lunches perfect for the beach, a long drive, or for the plane. Desserts include "The Famous Banana Split" and "To Die For Hana-Bars Sundae." Wireless Internet available here, too. Located in a small strip mall, **Honokowai Okazuya & Deli (34) ($)** *(3600 Lower Honoapiilani Rd. #D, Lahaina, 808-665-0512, M–Sa 10AM–2:30PM, 4:30PM–9PM)* is a hidden gem, serving mostly take-out plate lunches, sandwiches, salads, vegetarian items, and more. The quality and freshness rivals top-dollar restaurants in Lahaina. Beachfront **Sea House Restaurant (35) ($-$$)** *(Napili Kai Beach Resort, 5900 Lower Honoapi'ilani Rd., Lahaina, 808-669-1500, www.napilikai.com, daily 7AM–9PM)* has been a favorite for generations. The breakfasts are legendary. *Honolua (kalua* pork topped with cheddar polenta, eggs, and tomato vegetable sauce) and Moloka'i sweet potato egg frittata win raves. Lunch and dinner menus are sourced locally, offering everything from fresh sushi to grilled tofu. A three-course early bird dinner is available, too (place your order by 6PM). **Sansei Seafood Restaurant & Sushi Bar (36) ($-$$)** *(Kapalua Resort, 600 Office Rd., Lahaina, 808-669-6286, www.sanseihawaii.com/location. html, dinner 5:30PM–10PM, late-night dining Th–F 5:30PM–1AM)* also has locations in Kihei and on other islands; the menu features fresh sushi and specialties such as its panko-crusted ahi roll.

Bars, Nightlife, & *Lu'aus*:

The folks who brought you celebrated Maui restaurants **Pacific'O (26)** and **I'O (27)** *(see page 112)* present the lavish **Feast at Lele (37) ($$$$)** *(505 Front St., Lahaina, 866-244-5353, www.feastatlele.com, daily 6PM–9PM).* Guests are seated at linen-topped tables while servers bring out drinks and courses of small plates; the gourmet interpretations of Polynesian foods are well thought out and beautifully presented. Entertainment ranges from elegant Hawaiian hulas to a New Zealand haka war dance. It's a feast for eye, ear, and palate. A popular tradition, the award-winning **Old Lahaina Luau (38) ($$$$)** *(1251 Front St., Lahaina, 808-667-1998 or 800-248-5828, www.oldlahainaluau.com, nightly Apr–Sept 5:45PM, Oct.–Mar 5:15PM)* celebrates Hawaiian music, dance, and food. Guests receive a *lei* greeting and a cocktail and are led to a buffet, where they can choose from dozens of dishes, including *kalua* pig brought from the *imu* (underground oven) and desserts. Diners then settle under the stars to hear live music and watch hula performances.

Newly remodeled **Maui Brewing Co. Brewpub (39) ($-$$)** *(Kahana Gateway Center, 4405 Honoapiilani Hwy., Lahaina, 808-669-FISH [3474], http://mauibrewingco. com, daily 11AM–1AM)* is the restaurant arm of Maui's local brewery. The food is tasty, the beer is excellent, and they have a good wine selection, too. The soul and

sound of the islands, Grammy-winning **Masters of Hawaiian Slack Key Guitar (40)** *(888-669-3858, www. slackkey.com, check Web site for schedule)* perform regularly at the **Napili Kai Beach Resort (48)** *(see page 118)*. Performers "talk story" between numbers. Don't miss this entertaining, authentic Hawaiian music experience.

WHERE TO SHOP

On Lahaina's Front Street, treasure hunters have beaucoup galleries, tourist shops, and better boutiques to explore. Among the best: Banyan Tree Gallery (41) *(648 Wharf St. in the Old Lahaina Courthouse at Banyan Court, 808-661-0111, www.lahaina-arts.org, daily 9AM–5PM)*, run by the non-profit Lahaina Arts Society, and Village Galleries (42) *(120 Dickenson St., 808-661-4402, www.villagegalleriesmaui.com, hours vary)*, Maui's oldest gallery, also showcasing local artists. In Lahaina on Friday, stay for **Lahaina Art Night** *(along Front St., Lahaina, 808-661-0111, www.lahaina-arts.org, F 7PM–10PM)*; you'll have the opportunity to chat with artists and view and purchase their works—including paintings, prints, ceramics, art glass, handcrafted woodwork, scrimshaw, and jewelry. Martin Lawrence Galleries (43) *(Lahaina Marketplace, 126 Lahainaluna Rd., 808-661-1788, http://martinlawrence.com, daily 10AM–10PM)* offers works by Andy Warhol, Keith Haring, Roy Lichtenstein, Marc Chagall, Pablo Picasso, Joan Miró, and other artists.

Whalers Village (44) *(2435 Ka'anapali Pkwy., Lahaina, www.whalersvillage.com, daily 9:30AM–10PM)* is an upscale shopping center, with restaurants and retailers such as Louis Vuitton. If you go, check out **Lahaina Printsellers** *(1013 Limahana Pl., Lahaina, 808-667-5815 or 800-669-7843, www.printsellers.com, daily 9AM-10PM)*, a fascinating shop that displays and sells antique maps, charts, prints, engravings, and more.

Maui's Own Gift & Craft Fair (45) *(outside Lahaina Civic Center, 1840 Honoapi'ilani Hwy., Lahaina, 808-877-3100, www.mauiexposition.com/mauisown.html, Su throughout the year, 9AM–2PM, call for schedule updates)* is a local and visitor favorite for arts, crafts, food, and fun.

Across from **Honokowai Beach Park (14)**, **Honokowai Market (46)** *(3636 Lower Honoapi'ilani Rd., Honokowai, 808-669-7004, M, W, F 7AM–11AM)* offers fresh-from-the-farm produce and baked goods.

WHERE TO STAY

If luxury is on your vacation planner, consider the **Hyatt Regency Maui Resort & Spa (47)** **($$$)** *(200 Nohea Kai Dr., Lahaina, 808-661-1234 or 800-554-9288, www. maui.hyatt.com)*. The lobby soars skyward from a garden of exotic plants; swimming pools feature grottoes, caves, waterfalls, and a 150-foot slide. Top-of-the-line restaurants and cafés await your patronage. There's a "Drums of the Pacific" *lu'au*, too.

Tours introduce guests to on-site wildlife, art, and gardens, Camp Hyatt keeps kids busy, and a hotel-roof astronomy show wows everyone nightly. Why leave?

A great place to start a family tradition, **Napili Kai Beach Resort (48) ($$$)** *(5900 Lower Honoapi'ilani Rd., Lahaina, 808-669-6271 or 800-367-5030, www. napilikai.com)* is one of Maui's original resorts. Adults who came here as children return to enjoy its family-friendly suites and amenities, such as its free meet-and-greet Wednesday mai tai parties and its 10AM coffee klatches (announced by the blowing of a conch shell).

Grammy-winning **Masters of the Slack Key Guitar (40)** performers provide entertainment, as do students from the resort's own foundation school established to keep Hawaiian dance, music, and culture alive. Accommodations range from rooms and studios with bath, *lanai*, refrigerator, and coffee maker to two- and three-bedroom adjoining suites.

Landmark **Pioneer Inn (49) ($$)** *(658 Wharf St., Lahaina, 808-661-3636, www.pioneerinnmaui.com)*, the oldest hotel on Maui, has hosted such guests as Jack London and Jackie Onassis. Spencer Tracy and Frank Sinatra stayed here while filming 1961 volcano disaster flick *The Devil at Four O'clock*. And the inn inspired author Tom Robbins' novel *Still Life with Mockingbirds*. Though now managed by Best Western, the inn retains its early-1900s ambience, and is a stop on Lahaina's historical walking tour. Note: The inn is set right in the middle of the action here, so it may not the best choice for light sleepers.

Low-key "best value" Ka'anapali Beach Hotel (50) ($$-$$$) *(2525 Ka'anapali Pkwy., Lahaina, 808-661-0011 or 800-262-8450, www.kbhmaui.com)* routinely offers competitive room rates and packages (including airline discounts) and prides itself on being awarded the title "Most Hawaiian Hotel." Employees undergo a special program in Hawaiian history, customs, and hospitality, and the hotel offers an assortment of cultural activities.

A few blocks from town, Lahaina Shores (51) ($$-$$$) *(475 Front St., Lahaina, 808-661-4835 or 800-642-6284, www.lahainashores.com)* is a plantation-style beachfront property. Rooms range from studios to one-bedroom units

to penthouses. Spacious one-bedroom corner condos are the best deal and can sleep a family. This end of town is relatively quiet at night; the feast at Lele *lu'au* next door quiets down around 10PM. After that, all you hear is rolling surf. Maui Beachfront Rentals (52) ($-$$$$) *(256 Papalaua St., Lahaina, 808-661-3500 or 888-661-7200, www.mauibeachfront.com)* manages dozens of properties in a range of prices. Resort Quest Kaanapali Villas (53) ($$-$$$) *(45 Kai Ala Dr., Lahaina, 808-667-7791 or*

 *877-997-6667, www.rqkaana palivillas.com)* are located at the quiet north end of Ka'anapali Beach. The property has extensive land-scaped grounds and three swimming pools; accommodations include studios and suites with kitchens, and rooms with mini-refrigerators.

Just two blocks from the waterfront, boutique B&B **Plantation Inn (54) ($$-$$$)** *(174 Lahainaluna Rd., Lahaina, 808-667-9225 or 800-433-6815, www.the plantationinn.com)* combines Victorian-esque style with modern amenities: air conditioning, wireless Internet, soundproofing, pool, and Jacuzzi, as well as Mobile four-star French restaurant **Gerard's ($$-$$$) (28)** *(see page 112).*

Inviting **Old Lahaina House Bed & Breakfast (55) ($)** *(407 Ilikahi St., Lahaina, 808-667-4663 or 800-847-0761, www.oldlahaina.com)* offers great value, considering its convenient location and enclosed courtyard swimming pool. Lodgings include rooms with twin, queen, and king beds, and a suite. The innkeepers can also provide accommodation upgrades, add-ons, and rental cars (including a Lahaina-only two-seater electric car). **House of Fountains (56) ($$)** *(1579 Lokia St., Lahaina, 808-667-2121 or 800-789-6865, www.alohahouse.com)* B&B is located in a quiet residential neighborhood above Lahaina. Furnished with handmade koa wood furniture and Hawaiian quilts and artifacts, this attractive villa offers rooms, studios, and suites, as well as a pool and Jacuzzi. Guests wake up to a breakfast of fresh fruit, baked goods, and Kona coffee.

Bargain-priced **Camp Olowalu (57) ($)** *(800 Olowalu Rd., Olowalu, 6 mi. east of Lahaina, 808-661-4303, www. campolowalu.com)* offers 36 tent-camping spaces, and rents camping gear. It also has six plantation-style cabins furnished with cots with mattresses, a storage loft, a fan, electrical outlet, and screened windows with shutters. Cooking facilities and bathrooms are shared.

Hawaii is not a state of mind,
but a state of grace.

Paul Theroux

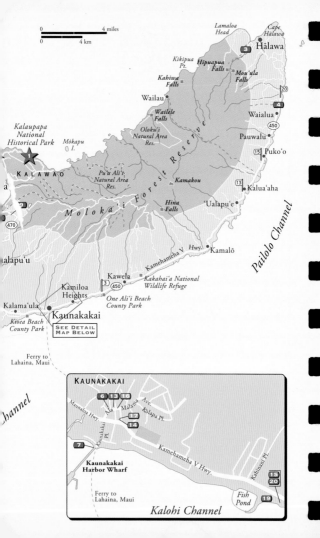

MOLOKA'I

PACIFIC OCEAN

Kahi'
Pt.

**Kalaupapa
Airport (LUP)**

8

Kalaupa

*Pālā'au
State Par*

10
12
13

11

Maunaloa Hwy.

*Pauahaia
Pt.*

Farrington Ave.

Mo'omomi Ave.

Puupeelua Ave.

Kalae St.

Kalae Hwy.

465

K

**Moloka'i
Airport (MKK)**

460

Maunaloa Hwy.

• Mo'omomi

*Mokio
Pt.*

Mahana •

Pu'u Nānā

*'Ilio
Pt.*

Kaluko'i Rd.

460

5

• Wahilauhue

Pohakuloa Rd.

Maunaloa

Kaiwi Channel

Kalohi

• Hālena

*Hale o Lono
Harbor*

• Kamāka'ipō

*Lā'au
Pt.*

| 5 | Mile marker

chapter 6

MOLOKA'I

MOLOKA'I

What to See:
1. KALAUPAPA NATIONAL HISTORIC PARK ★
2. Pala'au State Park
3. Halawa Valley

What to Do:
4. Waialua Beach
5. Papohaku Beach Park
6. Molokai Fish and Dive
7. Moloka'i Outdoors
8. Damien Tours
9. Moloka'i Mule Ride
10. Coffees of Hawaii Plantation Tours
11. Purdy's Natural Macadamia Nuts

Places to Eat & Drink:
12. Coffees of Hawaii Espresso Bar & Café
13. Kanemitsu Bakery
14. Molokai Drive-Inn
15. Hula Shores

Where to Shop:
16. Ala Malama Avenue
17. Molokai Fine Arts Gallery
18. Coffees of Hawaii Gift Shop

Where to Stay:
19. Marc Molokai Shores
20. Hotel Molokai
5. Papohaku Beach Park
2. Pala'au State Park

★ *Top Picks*

MOLOKA'I

• SNAPSHOT •

Moloka'i is nothing if not dramatic. Its western half is near desert; its north and east are covered by rain forest. Moloka'i was formed from three volcanoes: east-island Kamakou, the tallest at nearly 5,000 feet; western *Mauna Loa* ("Long Mountain"), rising to almost 1,400 feet; and a smaller third volcano which created the Makanalua Peninsula on the north shore. Moloka'i boasts the highest sea cliffs in the world (you can see them in the film *Jurassic Park III*) and the longest coral reef in the United States. Part of *Maui nui* (greater Maui), the island is managed as part of Maui County,

 with one exception—its geographically isolated Kalaupapa Peninsula, Kalawao County, now a national historic park. This is the historic site of a colony for people afflicted with Hansen's disease, or leprosy, an ailment cured in the 1940s.

Though this is a good-sized island (fifth largest in the Hawaiian chain), fewer than 7,500 people live here, mostly natives. Moloka'i considers itself the most "Hawaiian" island, and its residents are determined to remain unscathed by development. What makes Moloka'i, like Lana'i *(see page 136)*, special is what it is *not*: crowded, commercial, and convenient.

GETTING TO MOLOKA'I

By Air

You'll fly to Moloka'i via interisland or commuter flight, most likely from the Main Overseas Terminal building of O'ahu's **Honolulu International (HNL)** *(808-836-6413, 300 Rodgers Blvd. #4, Honolulu, www6.hawaii.gov/dot/airports/hnl). (See page 12 for more information.)* Centrally located **Moloka'i Airport (MKK)** *(access roads connected to Keonelele Ave., Hoolehua, 808-567-6361, www6.hawaii.gov/dot/airports/molokai/mkk)* primarily serves commuter planes. Several car rental companies service this airport. Moloka'i's **Kalaupapa Airport (LUP)** *(808-567-6106, Kalaupapa, www6.hawaii.gov/dot/airports/molokai/lup)* is really more of an airstrip on the island's northern peninsula, and is served by **Pacific Wings' Pacific Express Service** *(888-866-5022, www.pacificwings.com/pwexpress).*

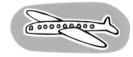

By Ferry

Moloka'i Ferry *(866-307-6524, www.molokaiferry.com)* offers twice-daily ferry service between Lahaina, Maui, and Kaunakakai Harbor, Moloka'i. Travel time is about two hours each way. Reservations are recommended. Note: Ferries are island residents' main source of transport for themselves and for personal goods; you may find ferries packed with natives' boxes, bags, tools, and equipment.

125

GETTING AROUND MOLOKA'I

Aloha Rents *(888-318-3307, www.aloharents.com, daily 6:30AM–7PM)* offers Dollar and Budget rentals at Moloka'i Airport. Note: They close after the day's last flight. **Island Kine Auto Rental** *(242 Ilio Rd.,Kaunakakai, 808-553-5242 or 877-553-5242, www.molokai-car-rental.com, daily 7AM–7PM)* will pick you up at the airport or wharf and drive you to your flight or ferry after you return your vehicle.

Twenty-four-hour taxi service on Moloka'i is available through **Hele Mai** ("Let's Go") **Taxi** *(808-336-0967 or 808-646-9060)* to and from the airport, harbor, and Kaunakakai. Other destinations upon request; they also offer private island tours.

VISITOR INFORMATION

For information on visiting Moloka'i, contact the **Moloka'i Visitors Association** *(2 Kamoi St., Ste. 200, Kaunakakai, HI 96748, 808-553-3876, 808-553-5221, or 800-800-6367, www.molokai-hawaii.com)*, or contact the **Hawaii Visitors and Convention Bureau** *(800-GOHAWAII [464-2924], www.gohawaii.com)*.

WHAT TO SEE

TOP PICK!

The only word to describe ★**KALAUPAPA NATIONAL HISTORIC PARK (1)** *(808-567-6802, www.nps.gov/kala, entry by reservation only through Damien Tours, 808-567-6171, or Moloka'i Mule Ride, see below)* is "beautiful," in both a physical and a spiritual sense. Set on a remote peninsula crowned by a dormant volcano with a lake hundreds of feet deep, Kalaupapa ("Flat Leaf," after the peninsula's shape as seen from above) was for centuries home to ancient  Hawaiians who lived off the bounty of the land and sea. The area came to the attention of the world in 1866, when the last Hawaiian king of the Kamehameha lineage chose to banish those with leprosy, a then-incurable disease, to this isolated place. It's believed more than 8,000 people were exiled here over the years. Separated from the rest of the island by a sheer 1,700-foot *pali*, or cliff, the colony was a frightening place of degradation and predation. In 1873, a Belgian priest named Father Damien chose to serve the populace here. He restored order and created a community with the help of the inhabitants themselves and others, including Franciscan nun Mother Marianne Cope. Norwegian doctor Gerhard Hansen isolated the bacteria for the disease in 1873, though effective treatment via sulfa drugs wasn't available until the 1940s. Further medical advancements have rendered the disease incommunicable, and those with Hansen's disease (the preferred term) live normal lives. Still, about two dozen residents remain in Kalaupapa today by choice. Park visits are arranged solely through **Damien Tours (8)** *(see page 129)*. The famous **Moloka'i Mule Ride (9)** *(see page 130)* is an unforgettable way to get there.

A cool, forested park located atop the pali, **Pala'au State Park (2)** *(end of Kalae Hwy./Hwy. 470, Pala'au, 808-567-6923, www.hawaiistateparks.org)* over-looks the Makanalua Peninsula and Kalalupapa. There are several trails here, including one leading to Kauleonanahoa, or "Phallic Rock,"

once a destination for women hoping to conceive.

The **Halawa Valley (3)** *(northeast Moloka'i , 30 miles from Kaunakakai via Hwy. 450, open for guided tours only)* is home to several ancient Hawaiian *heiaus* (worship sites). **Molokai Fish and Dive (6)** and **Moloka'i Outdoors (7)** *(see next page)* can provide escorted treks to this "cathedral valley," once completely closed to the public. The approximately four mile, round-trip rainforest trail fol-lows a stream from the sea up into the valley. You'll ford waterways, clamber over slippery rocks, and take in two dramatic waterfalls and a pool in which you may be able to swim, depending on water flow (and the mood of the legendary giant lizard, or *mo'o*, who sleeps beneath).

WHAT TO DO
Beaches:

The smaller waves at eastern Moloka'i 's **Waialua Beach (4)** *(mile marker 19, Kamehameha V Hwy./Hwy. 450, east of Kaunakakai, no phone, open daily)* make this a pleasant spot for swimmers, snorkelers, and beginning surfers. On the island's west end, Honolulu glows at night from across Kaiwi Channel at gorgeous **Papohaku**

Beach Park (5) *(mile 14.9, Kaluako'i Rd., 808-553-3204, www.co.maui.hi.us/index.asp?NID=287, open daily, no lifeguard)*. The usually uncrowded three-mile expanse is one of the state's biggest beaches. Note: Trade winds buffet the beach, especially in winter. Use extreme care when swimming. Wind-blown sand sometimes makes sunbathing uncomfortable. Parking, picnic facilities, showers, restrooms, and water are available.

Watersports & More Activities:

Tours at **Molokai Fish and Dive (6)** *(61 Ala Malama Ave., Kaunakakai, 808-553-5926, www.molokaifishanddive. com, daily 7:30AM–6PM)* cover everything from sea kayaking to fishing to cultural hikes. You can pick up rental equipment here, as well as locally-designed T-shirts and souvenirs, books, Hawaiian shirts, straw hats, and much more. **Moloka'i Outdoors (7)** *(Kaunakakai Harbor Port, 808-553-4477 or 877-553-4477, www. molokai-outdoors.com, office hours:*

M–Sa 8AM–10AM, 4PM–6PM) facilitates tours and activities (from hikes to horseback rides), provides vehicle and equipment rentals (from tennis rackets and surf boards to kayaks and bicycles), and can arrange accommodation packages for visitors.

Access to the **Kalaupapa National Historical Park (1)** is available only through **Damien Tours (8)** *(advance reservations required, call 808-567-6171)*. Tour guide Richard Marks acquaints visitors with historic churches, cemeteries, monuments to Father Damien and Mother Cope, and other highlights, including a visitor center in the Americans of Japanese Ancestry Buddhist Hall. Visitors *must* contact Damien Tours beforehand to make a reservation and arrange pickup at trail's end. You can either hike the trail or sign up for the famous mule ride *(see below)*. Thinking about hiking it? Keep in mind that many of the 26 switchback turns have fairly steep drops between steps, so the hike is recommended only for those with sturdy knees and hips. Hikers are also advised to start before 8AM to beat the mule riders *(next listing)* down the cliff.

The Damien tour is included for those opting to spend a day with one of the smart, sure-footed friends of **Moloka'i Mule Ride (9)** *(mile marker 5, Kala'e Hwy./Hwy. 470, Kualapuu, 808-567-6088, or 800-567-7550, reserve at least 2 weeks in advance, ages 16–up, 250 lbs. and under, www.muleride.com, check-in M–Sa 8AM)*. This six-mile, seven-hour experience takes riders down the world's highest sea cliffs through pretty **Pala'au State Park (2)** into **Kalaupapa National Historical Park (1)** and back again. The mellow, well-trained equines navigate the switchback turns with ease. Ride includes entry permits, light lunch, park fees, Damien historical tour *(see above)*, and certificate of completion. This is an unforgettable way to experience the Kalaupapa Trail.

Wake up and smell the oh-so-delicious aromas at **Coffees of Hawaii Plantation Tours (10)** *(1630 Farrington Ave. off Rte. 470, Kualapuʻu, 808-567-9490 or 877-322-3276, www.coffeesofhawaii.com, M–F 6AM–5PM, Sa 8AM–4PM, Su 8AM–7PM)*. Take a walking "Morning Espresso Tour" *(M–F 10AM & 2PM, Sa 9AM)* or a two-hour mule-drawn wagon tour *(M–F 9AM & 1PM, Sa 8AM)*. Or stop in for a self-guided afternoon hike *(M–F 3:30PM–5PM)* through the fields to the top of Kualapuʻu Hill. At **Purdy's Natural Macadamia Nuts (11)** *(Lihi Pali Ave., Hoʻolehua, 2 miles west of Kualapuʻu, 808-567-6601, http://molokai-aloha.com/macnuts, M–F 9:30AM–3:30PM, Sa 10AM–2PM, Su by appointment)*, visitors can tour a working macadamia nut farm and buy fresh raw and roasted nuts, macadamia nut honey, and other products.

PLACES TO EAT & DRINK

Sip a robust coffee drink, or enjoy sweet pastry, shave ice, or a sandwich at the **Coffees of Hawaii Espresso Bar & Café (12) ($)** *(Coffees of Hawaii Plantation, 1630 Farrington Ave., Kualapu'u, 808-567-9490, ext. 27, www. coffeesofhawaii.com, M–F 7AM–4PM, Sa 8AM–4PM, Su 8AM–2PM).*

Sugar? Butter? You can never have enough! Family-owned **Kanemitsu Bakery (13) ($)** *(79 Ala Malama Ave., Kaunakakai, 808-553-5855, W–M 5:30AM–6:30PM, fresh bread may be purchased from the night baker out back after 10:30PM)* has been baking good things for decades. Their breads are irresistible, and beware those innocent looking yellow-topped muffins. Breakfasts and lunches served here, too, until early afternoon. At some point, everyone winds up at island mainstay **Molokai Drive-Inn (14) ($)** *(15 Kamoi St., corner Kamehameha V Hwy./Rte. 450, Kaunakakai, 808-553-5655, daily 6AM–10PM).* At night, it looms out of the darkness like a squat green ghost, offering everything from Spam and shakes to fresh fish plates, at prices straight out of the 1960s. Skip the burgers and go directly for the fish and BLTs. Good breakfasts, too.

The view is impressive and the menu ambitious at open-air **Hula Shores (15) ($-$$)** *(Hotel Molokai, just before mile marker 2, Kamehameha V Hwy./Hwy. 450, Kaunakakai, 808-553-5347 or 800-535-0085, www.hotelmolokai.*

com, daily 7AM–10:30AM, 11AM–2PM, dinner 6PM–9PM, F 4PM–9PM), all day, every day. It serves up tasty breakfasts and lunchtime sandwiches and salads, and it really shines for dinner, especially with the day's fresh catch and *paniolo*-style pork ribs. There's a full bar and live ukulele and slack key guitar music, too. Stop by for the "Aloha Friday Sunset Celebration."

WHERE TO SHOP

Step back in time to the days of *aloha* along three-block Ala Malama Avenue (16) *(Kaunakakai)*, the "hub" of the town, with Old West, Boomtown-style false front buildings and eclectic cafés and shops. Acclaimed Molokai Fine Arts Gallery (17) *(2 Kamoi St., Ste. 300, Kaunakakai, 808-553-8520, http://molokaifinearts.com, hours vary, call ahead)* presents works by dozens of Moloka'i artists: paintings, photographs, carved and turned wood, Hawaiian quilts, jewelry, and much more.

Coffees of Hawaii Plantation Gift Shop (18) *(Coffees of Hawaii Plantation, 1630 Farrington Ave., Kualapu'u, 808-567-9490 ext. 26, www.coffeesofhawaii.com, M–F 8AM–5PM, Sa 8AM–4PM, Su 8AM–2PM)* sells coffees by the pound, as well as a variety of authentic Hawaiian gifts and goods.

WHERE TO STAY

Marc Molokai Shores (19) ($$) *(just before mile marker 2, Kamehameha V Hwy./Hwy. 450, Kaunakakai, 808-553-5954, www.marcresorts.com)* offers condos with kitchen

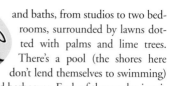

and baths, from studios to two bedrooms, surrounded by lawns dotted with palms and lime trees. There's a pool (the shores here don't lend themselves to swimming) and barbecues. Each of the condos is privately owned, so upgrades vary: ask for what you want (ground floor, quiet, etc.). Next door, Polynesian-styled **Hotel Molokai (20) ($$)** *(just before mile marker 2, Kamehameha V Hwy./Hwy. 450, Kaunakakai, 808-553-5347 or 800-535-0085, www.hotelmolokai.com)* features recently updated rooms in a cluster of two-story buildings on the ocean. Note: Though some rooms have ocean views, the shoreline here is not swimmable; the hotel has a pool, however. Amenities include high-speed Internet access, cable TV, compact refrigerators, private *lanais*, and fans (which cool the air better than air conditioning in this climate). Some rooms have kitchenettes. Rooms upstairs are a little larger. Like to retire early? Ask for a room away from the hotel's open-air **Hula Shores (15)** *(see page 132)* restaurant, which may get boisterous, especially on weekends.

Camping is allowed at **Papohaku Beach Park (5)**; obtain permits from the **Mitchell Pauole Community Center** *(Aiona St. & Ala Malama Ave., Kaunakakai, 808-553-3204, M–F 8AM–4PM)*. You may also camp at **Pala'au State Park (2)** *(end of Kala'e Hwy./Hwy. 470, Pala'au, 808-567-6923, www.hawaiistateparks.org)*.

Obtain a camping permit prior to your trip from the park office *(Hwy. 470, 808-567-6923)* or district office *(Division of State Parks, 54 S. High St., Rm. 101, Wailuku, HI 96793, 808-984-8109, details on state park permits and fees at www.hawaiistateparks.org/camping/fees.cfm)*. There is a restroom, but you must bring your own water.

A day without *aloha* is just another mainland day.

Buck Buchanan

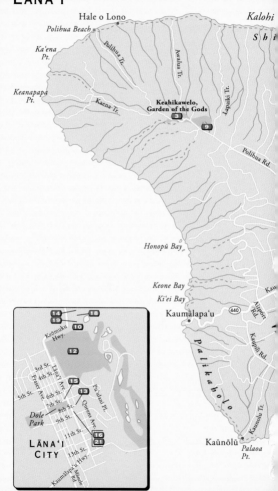

LĀNA'I

Hale o Lono

Polihua Beach

Ka'ena Pt.

Keanapapa Pt.

Kalohi

Sh i

Polihua Tr.

Awalua Tr.

Lapaiki Tr.

Kaena Tr.

**Keahikawelo,
Garden of the Gods**

3

9

Polihua Rd.

Honopū Bay

Keone Bay

Ki'ei Bay

Kaumālapa'u

440

Airport Rd.

Kaupili Rd.

Kaumolu Tr.

Pali kaholo

Kau

Kaunōlū

*Palaoa
Pt.*

LĀNA'I CITY

14

19

18

10

Keōmuku Hwy.

12

3rd St.

4th St.

5th St.

6th St.

Lāna'i Ave.

Fraser Ave.

15

7th St.

8th St.

Dole Park

9th St.

11th St.

13

Pu'uhai Pl.

Queens Ave.

16

21

13th St.

Kaumālapa'u Hwy.

Kaumālapa'u Maile Rd.

chapter 7

LANAʻI

LANA'I

What to See:

What to Do:

Places to Eat & Drink:

Where to Stay:

★ *Top Picks*

LANA'I

• SNAPSHOT •

With two top-tier luxury hotels, a pair of spectacular golf courses, equally spectacular snorkeling opportunities, and a small city populated mostly by natives, the lovely island of Lana'i is the place to go for rest, relaxation, recreation, and exclusivity. Like Moloka'i, Lana'i is part of *Maui nui* (greater Maui), albeit smaller in ter-

 ritory and roughly half the population of Moloka'i. Pineapple purveyor James Dole bought the entire island in 1922 for cultivation. (Note: Though pineapples are indelibly associated with Hawaii, they are actually native to South America. Dole experimented with different strains to find varieties that would thrive in volcanic soil.)

Dole's company was purchased by developer Castle & Cooke in the early 1960s; over the years, the focus turned from farming to tourism, but the native Lana'ians who spend their days working for the island's hotels and their guests follow an age-old lifestyle based on hunting, fishing, and family. Lana'i City, the island's sole town, has a small commercial area surrounding Dole Park, one gas station, and few paved roads. Many visitors come as day-trippers to snorkel in pristine, protected Hulopo'e Bay. Those exploring beyond the hotels must do so on dirt roads via tours and/or rented four-wheel-drive vehicles.

GETTING TO LANA‘I

By Air

You'll fly to Lana‘i via interisland or commuter flight, most likely from the Main Overseas Terminal building of O‘ahu's **Honolulu International (HNL)** *(808-836-6413, 300 Rodgers Blvd. #4, Honolulu, www6.hawaii.gov/ dot/airports/hnl). (See page 12 for more information.)* **Lana‘i Airport (LNY)** *(access roadway from Kaumalapau Hwy., Lana‘i City, 808-565-6757, www6.hawaii. gov/dot/airports/lanai/lny)* is a commuter strip between Manele Bay Harbor and Lana‘i City. Free shuttle service is available to hotel guests; others can catch the Lana‘i City shuttle.

By Ferry

Lana‘i Ferry's *Expeditions* *(800-695-2624, www.go- lanai.com)* provides ferry service several times a day between Lahaina, Maui, and Manele Bay, Lana‘i. The crossing takes about 45 minutes. Tip: The trip is easier on calm morning seas; it often takes longer late in the day when the water gets choppy. Reservations recom- mended.

GETTING AROUND LANA‘I

Renting a four-wheel-drive vehicle is the only option if you want to explore Lana‘i beyond the village and paved roads. Rental companies will give directions, maps, and practical advice for driving dirt and gravel roads. Tips: Don't drive in inclement weather. Make sure you have a full tank of gas. Bring water and food. In Lana'i, the **Dollar Rent-a-Car** office *(located at Lana'i City Service, 1036 Lana'i Ave., Lana'i City, 800-533-7808 or 808-565-7227, www.dollar.com)* is the place to go for a car or a four-wheel-drive vehicle. Another option for airport or ferry pickup: **Adventure Lana'i Ecocentre (13)** *(338 8th St., Lana'i City, 808-565-7373, www.adventurelanai.com) (also see page 143)*, offering Safari Jeep or Land Rover rentals for off-road exploring.

VISITOR INFORMATION

For information on Lana'i, contact the **Lana'i Visitors Bureau** *(mailing address: P.O. Box 631436, Lana'i City, HI 96763, location: 431 7th Ave., Ste. A, Lana'i City, 800-947-4774 or 808-565-7600, www.visitlanai.net)* or the **Hawaii Visitors and Convention Bureau** *(800-GOHAWAII [464-2924], www.gohawaii.com)*.

WHAT TO SEE

TOP PICK!

★**HULOPO'E BAY (1)** *(Hwy. 440 & Manele Rd. south to Hulopo'e Beach Park)* splashes out onto a picture-perfect, often deserted white sand beach, but the real draw here is the bay itself. This Marine Life Conservation District is restricted from powerboats and invasive diving. A pod of spinner dolphins resides here; swimmers may enjoy their antics from a distance. (Dolphins are protected and are not to be approached.) You'll be too busy saying "wow" into your snorkel tube to care; this snorkeler's paradise teems with tropical fish and some of the most colorful coral you'll see outside an aquarium. Schools of yellow tang dart over a sea bottom that looks as though a clumsy painter knocked over buckets of blue, pink, and lavender. As always, beware changes in weather and strong currents and swells.

Also part of the Manele-Hulopo'e Marine Life Conservation District, **Manele Bay (2)** *(Hwy. 440 & Manele Rd. south to Manele Beach Park)* is a short walk from Hulopo'e Beach. The bay is the docking place for ferries and *Trilogy* tours from Lahaina *(see page 109)*. West of the bay, divers thrill to the famous **Cathedrals** *(accessible by boat)*, towering underwater pinnacles that serve as home to an amazing diversity of marine life.

Keahikawelo (3) *(Polihua Rd., about 7 miles northwest of Lana'i City, 800-947-4774, www.visitlanai.net)*, "fire of Kawelo," popularly known as **Garden of the Gods**, is a twisted landscape of wild, wind-scoured rock formations, lava flows, and bands of striated colors that are especially vivid at sunset. Treacherous rocks, reefs, and currents created eerie, eight-mile-long **Shipwreck Beach (4)** *(northeast side of island, 800-947-4774, www.visit lanai.net)*, where the rusting hulk of the 1949s tanker *Liberty* looms. You'll find some of Lana'i's famed **petroglyphs** nearby *(off Keomuku Hwy.; ask your vehicle rental agency for specific directions)*. South of the city, a dirt and

gravel track leads to the Luahiwa Petroglyphs (5) *(off Manele Rd.)*. Make sure you get exact directions to the site from your rental agency, as the journey requires navigating poorly marked roads and moderate to difficult hiking.

WHAT TO DO
Beaches:

Separated by a volcanic cone, **Hulopo'e Beach Park (6)** and adjacent **Manele Beach Park (7)** *(take Hwy. 440 south from Lana'i City, http://hawaii.gov/dlnr/dar/coral/mlcd_ manele.html, open daily)* afford excellent summer swimming, snorkeling, and whale and dolphin watching in season. Facilities include picnic tables, grills, restrooms, and showers.

Hiking:

The **Munro Trail (8)** *(leaving Hwy. 440 about ½ mi. north of Lana'i City, 800-947-4774, www.visitlanai.net)* leads to Lana'i's highest point, 3,370-foot Mount Lana'ihale (most refer to it as "the hale"). The mountain lends thrilling views of all Hawaii's islands except Kaua'i and Ni'ihau. The trail, a seven-mile loop, passes through a series of dramatic gulches and a forest of Cook Island pines, eucalyptus trees, and ferns planted in the early 20th century by New Zealand naturalist George Munro. **Kanepu'u Reserve (9)** *(on the way to Keahikawelo, see page 141)* is a forest preserve with an easy quarter-mile loop hiking trail that winds among trees and plants native to the islands before the arrival of man.

Golf:

The larger hotels boast outstanding courses: the Greg Norman/Ted Robinson–designed **Experience at Koele (10)** *(Four Seasons Resort Lodge at Koele, 1 Keomoku Hwy., Lana'i City, 808-565-4653 or 800-565-4610, www.four seasons.com/manelebay/golf/the_experience_at_koele.html)* is surrounded by lush mountain scenery. Designed by Jack Nicklaus, the spectacular **Challenge at Manele (11)** *(Four Seasons Resort Lana'i at Manele Bay, 1 Manele Bay Rd., Lana'i City, 808-565-2000 or 800-321-4666 or 808-565-2222, www.fourseasons.com/manelebay/golf.html)* course is set on the sea cliffs above Hulopo'e Bay. The Pacific is your water hazard on three holes.

Built in 1947 for Dole corporation employees, nine-hole **Cavendish Golf Course (12)** *(Keomoku Rd. near the Lodge at Koele outside Lana'i City, 808-565-7300)* is open to the public by donation.

More Activities:

Adventure Lana'i Ecocentre (13) *(338 8th St., Lana'i City, 808-565-7373, www.adventurelanai.com) (also see page 140)* offers escorted ATV or Land Rover tours of island beach, forest, and ridge trails. They also rent vehicles and gear and provide tours/adventures/clinics for mountain biking, sea kayaking, snorkeling, and surfing. Discover the island on horseback through **Koele Stables (14)** *(Hwy. 440 north of Lana'i City, on the left past the Lodge at Koele, 808-565-4424, reservation required)*, providing a variety of relaxed rides, including trail, sunset, and children's rides.

PLACES TO EAT & DRINK

Warm, welcoming **Blue Ginger Café (15) ($)** *(409 7th St., Lana'i City, 808-565-6363, daily 6AM–8PM)* serves satisfying breakfasts, lunches, and dinners to visitors and locals. Expect ethnic dishes such as chicken katsu, plus plate lunches and fresh fish at prices that won't break the bank. The upscale offerings at **Lana'i City Grille (16) ($-$$)** *(Hotel Lana'i, 828 Lana'i Ave., Lana'i City, 808-565-7211, www.hotellanai.com, W–Su 5PM–9PM, reservations recommended)* were designed by award-winning chef Bev Gannon *(see also pages 77 & 93)* and include seafood and a signature rotisserie chicken. Friday nights, local talent entertains in the outdoor *lanai*.

The island's Four Seasons Resorts *(also see next page)* offer restaurants ranging from casual to formal, with prices to match. Menus incorporate island specialties, beautifully presented. Examples: Inviting, ocean-view **Hulopoe Court (17) ($$-$$$)** *(lower lobby level, Four Seasons Resort Lana'i at Manele Bay, 1 Manele Bay Rd., Lana'i City, 808-565-2000, daily 7AM–11AM, Sa–W 6PM–9:30PM, resort attire, www.fourseasons.com/manelebay/dining.html/)*, serving à la carte and buffet breakfast daily, as well as dinner several evenings a week, with a focus on Hawaiian-inspired Pacific Rim cuisine. Romantic **Dining Room (18) ($$$)** *(lobby level, Four Seasons Resort Lodge at Koele, 1 Keomoku Hwy., 808-565-4000, www.fourseasons.com/koele/dining/.html, daily 6PM–9:30PM, resort attire)*, offers estate ambiance, complete with fireplace, and artful new takes on culinary favorites.

WHERE TO STAY

The **Four Seasons Resort Lanai, The Lodge at Koele (19) ($$$$)** *(1 Keomoku Hwy., Lana'i City, 808-565-4000 or 800-321-4666, www.fourseasons.com/koele)*, exudes genteel, upcountry ambiance. Take afternoon tea and enjoy live evening entertainment in the Great Hall, which features two of the biggest fireplaces in Hawaii. The lodge offers multiple lounges and dining venues, a state-of-the-art fitness center and pool, spa services, tennis, golf, sporting clays and archery, and more. The **Four Seasons Resort Lana'i at Manele Bay (20) ($$$$)** *(1 Manele Bay Rd., Lana'i City, 808-565-2000 or 800-321-4666, www.fourseasons.com/manelebay)* takes its decorative themes from Mediterranean, Indian, Japanese, Chinese, and Hawaiian cultures. The spa offers a variety of treatments. A fitness center, a pool, restaurants, lounges, tennis, golf, a teen center, and other amenities cover all a visitor might require.

Charming **Hotel Lana'i (21) ($$)** *(828 Lana'i Ave., Lana'i City, 808-565-7211, www.hotellanai.com)*, built in 1923 for Dole pineapple executives, is a reasonably priced alternative for visitors.

There are six tent-only **Castle & Cooke Resorts campsites (22)** on Hulopo'e Bay (1) *(available by reservation through Castle & Cooke Resorts, P.O. Box 630310, Lana'i City, Lana'i, HI 96763, attn: Camping, or call 808-565-2970 at least 2–3 weeks in advance of your trip)*, with nice placement for privacy. Facilities include restrooms, outdoor showers, grills, picnic tables, and drinking water.

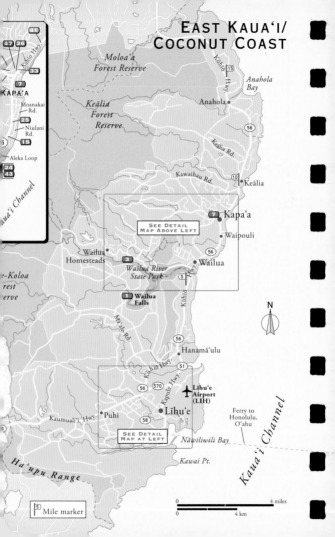

EAST KAUA'I/
COCONUT COAST

SEE DETAIL
MAP ABOVE LEFT

SEE DETAIL
MAP AT LEFT

Moloa'a
Forest Reserve

Anahola
Bay

Keālia
Forest
Reserve

Anahola

Kūhiō Hwy. 15

Kūhiō Hwy.

KAPA'A

Moanakai
Rd.

Niulani
Rd.

Aleka Loop

ua'i Channel

Kawaihau Rd.

Keālia Rd.

56

10 Keālia

7 Kapa'a

Waipouli

56

Wailua
Homesteads

3

Wailua River
State Park

Wailua

5

-Koloa
rest
erve

Wailua
Falls

Mā'alo Rd.

Kūhiō Hwy.

56

Hanamā'ulu

Kūhiō Hwy.

56 570

Kapule Hwy.

51

Līhu'e
Airport
(LIH)

Puhi

Kaumuali'i Hwy.

58

Līhu'e

Ferry to
Honolulu,
O'ahu

Nāwiliwili Bay

Kawai Pt.

Ha'upu Range

Kaua'i Channel

N

5 Mile marker

0 ——————— 4 miles
0 ——————— 4 km

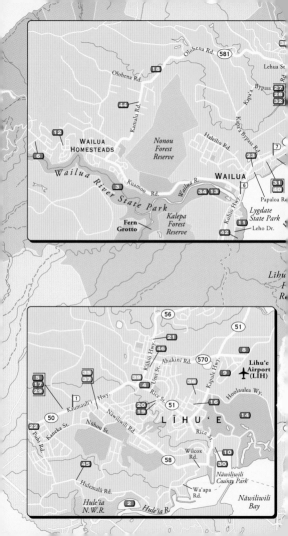

Map labels (top map — Wailua area):

Olohena Rd.

581

Lehua St

18

Olohena Rd.

Bypass 27
26
32

44 Kamalu Rd.

Kapa'a

Kapa'a Bypass Rd.

12

WAILUA
HOMESTEADS

Nonou
Forest
Reserve

Haleilio Rd.

7

6

Kuamo'o 3

Wailua River State Park

23

WAILUA

31
40

Wailua R.

34 13

Papaloa R

Kuamo'o
Rd.

6

Fern
Grotto

Kalepa
Forest
Reserve

Kūhiō Hwy.

Lygdate
State Park

11

42

Leho Dr.

Līhu
F
R

Map labels (bottom map — Līhu'e area):

56

51

21

8

46

Kūhiō Hwy.

Ahukini Rd.

570

Lihu'e
Airport
(LIH)

5
17
29

35
37

39

'Umi St.

Kapule Hwy.

9

Kaumuali'i Hwy.

Rice St.

36

16

50

Nāwiliwili Rd.

20
19

51

LĪHU'E

14

Hoolaulea Wy.

22

Puhi Rd.

Kaneka St.

Nuhou St.

Rice St.

Wilcox
Rd.

10

58

30

45

Hulemalū Rd.

Nāwiliwili
County Park

Hule'ia
N.W.R.

2

Wa'apa
Rd.

Hule'ia R.

Nāwiliwili
Bay

chapter 8

EAST KAUA'I/
COCONUT COAST

EAST KAUA'I/COCONUT COAST

What to See:
1. Wailua Falls
2. Menehune Fishpond
3. Wailua River State Park
4. Kaua'i Museum
5. Kilohana Plantation
6. Kauai Aadheenam Monastery
7. Kapa'a

What to Do:
8. Island Helicopters
9. Tropical Biplanes
10. Kalapaki Beach
11. Lydgate Beach Park
12. Wailua River Kayak Adventures
13. Smith's Fern Grotto Wailua River Cruise
14. Kauai Lagoons Golf Club
15. Hawaii Movie Tours
16. Polynesian Adventure Tours
17. Kauai Plantation Railway
18. Steelgrass Farm

Places to Eat & Drink:
19. Hamura Saimin Stand
20. Barbecue Inn
21. The Fish Express
22. Hanalima Baking
23. Kintaro
24. Hukilau Lanai
25. Aloha Diner
26. Mermaids Café
27. Blossoming Lotus
28. Lotus Root Juice Bar
29. Gaylord's Restaurant
30. Nawiliwili Tavern
31. Hula Girl Bar and Grill
32. Lotus Lounge
33. Pizzetta
34. Smith Family Garden Lu'au

Where to Shop:
35. Kukui Grove Shopping Center
36. Sunshine Market
37. Kukui Grove Center Monday Market
38. Kapa'a Sunshine Market
39. Stitchery
40. Coconut MarketPlace
41. Kaua'i Products Fair

Where to Stay:

*Will you remember when you go away,
the fragrance of ginger blooms
in a white lei?*

Dan Blanding

● SNAPSHOT ●

Thanks to a determined local populace, Kaua'i has modernized but not lost its "Garden Isle" feel. You can shop at Wal-Mart and 20 minutes later have lunch at a fish store in a plantation town. A restriction on building height (no taller than a palm tree) has made a world of difference with regard to the landscape here.

The east end of Kaua'i, popularly known as the Coconut Coast, is the primary entry point to the island. Most arrive by air in the town of Lihu'e, the island's hub, with 5,000 residents and most of the stoplights (under ten). Cruise ships dock south of town in Nawiliwili Harbor. Old Lihu'e hasn't changed much through the years, though its surrounds now include suburbs, big box stores, and an upscale shopping center anchored by Macy's. Despite its being the center of commerce and government, Lihu'e retains its small-town charm and proximity to wilder places. Waterfalls and emerald-hued cane fields are within a few minutes' drive.

To the north, Kapa'a town is the crossroads of the island and a picturesque place to wander on foot.

Beware two local species gone wild: chickens and cats. The chickens are believed to be descended from farm-yard fowl set free during 1992's Hurricane Iniki. They roost in trees, roam the road, and are hard to catch (by humans anyway). The feral felines, on the other hand, seem to thrive on a diet of the pertinacious poultry.

GETTING TO KAUA'I

By Air

Nonstop flights are available through major carriers direct to Kaua'i. However, traveling via interisland or commuter flight from Honolulu *(see page 12 for more information)* to Kaua'i is worth checking out. There are also a few daily direct flights from Maui and the Big Island to Kaua'i. **Lihu'e Airport (LIH)** *(3901 Mokulele Loop, Lihu'e, 808-246-1448, www6.hawaii.gov/dot/ airports/kauai/lih)* is about two miles east of Lihu'e town. Major passenger airlines and commercial and cargo carriers use this airport. The **Port Allen Airport (PAK)** on Kaua'i's west side *(Ka'alani Rd., 808-246-1448, www6.hawaii.gov/dot/airports/kauai/pak)* is a single runway facility, mostly used by private aircraft and heli-copters. **Princeville Airport (HPV)** *(Princeville)* is a private airport in northern Kaua'i.

By Cruise Ship

The cruise lines that stop in Maui *(see page 31)* usually include a port of call in Kaua'i. Length of stay varies with the cruise chosen.

Driving is the easiest way to see Kaua'i. You'll find most leading car rental companies across from Lihu'e airport. It's smart to reserve a vehicle in advance during high season. Note: The major rental companies generally require that you be 25 years old and have a valid driver's license and credit card. Alternative **Island Cars** *(2983 Aukele St., Lihu'e, 800-246-6009 or 808-246-6000, www.island cars.net)* rents cars to those under 26 and/or without a major credit card.

You can also see the sights from a Harley; rent one from **Kaua'i Harley-Davidson** *(3-1866 Kaumuali'i Hwy., Lihu'e, 808-241-7020, www.kauai harley-davidson.com, daily 8AM–6PM)* or **Cycle City/Two Wheels** *(4555 Pouli Rd., Kapa'a, 808-822-7283, www. cyclecitykauai.com, M–F 9AM–6PM, Sa 9AM–5PM)*.

Kaua'i Bus *(808-241-6410, www.kauai.gov/Transportation, M–F 5:27AM–7:50PM, Sa 6:21AM–5:50PM, www.kauai. gov/Transportation)* takes passengers between Hanalei and Kekaha, and provides service to Lihu'e Airport and limited service to Koloa and Poipu.

There are a number of cab companies on Kaua'i, including **South Shore Taxi and Limo** *(Koloa, 808-742-1525, www.southshoretaxi.com)*, **North Shore Cab** *(808-639-7829, Kilauea, www.northshorecab.com)*, **Akiko's** *(Kapa'a, 808-822-7588)*, and **City Cab** *(Lihu'e, 808-245-3227)*.

VISITOR INFORMATION

For more information on visiting the "Garden Isle," contact the **Kaua'i Visitors Bureau** *(4334 Rice St., Ste. 101, Lihu'e, HI 96766, 808-245-3971 or 800-262-1400, www.kauaidiscovery.com or www.kauai-hawaii. com)* or the **Hawaii Visitors and Convention Bureau** *(800-GOHAWAII [464-2924], www.gohawaii.com)*.

WHAT TO SEE

Remember the waterfalls from the opening scenes of *Fantasy Island*? They're here on Kaua'i. High above the

cane fields, dramatic double **Wailua Falls (1)** *(end of Rte. 583/Ma'alo Rd., follow signs)* cascade over 80 feet to a pool below. Many of the surrounding trees are intertwined with morning glories, making the sight even more spectacular early in the day.

A fascinating example of ancient aquaculture, **Menehune Fishpond (2)** *(near the Hule'ia National Wildlife Refuge on Hulemalu Rd.)*, or **Alekoko Fishpond**, is a lake-like area enclosed by a 900-foot-long, five-foot-high wall of lava stones. Legend has it that the fishpond was built in one night by Hawaii's mythical *Menehune*, or little people. Though covered by greenery and under water, it's a construction job that evokes Stonehenge or the Easter Island statues. The fishpond was used to trap fish between Huleo Stream and **Nawiliwili Bay**. The area is especially beautiful close to sunset, but take care. The island's cheeky chickens roam the roads at dusk, and you may end up with one as a hood ornament

Poli'ahu Heiau in Wailua River State Park (3) *(historic sites & scenic overlooks on Kuamo'o Rd., Hwy. 580, 808-274-3444, www.hawaiistateparks.org/parks/Kauai, open daily during daylight hours)* is one of several ancient sites located along the road that runs parallel to the Wailua River. The park encompasses remains of *heiaus* (places of worship), *pu'uhonua* (places of refuge), and other structures at this once-important seat of royal power. The park also features scenic overlooks, waterfalls, and picnicking

areas. River excursions and guided tours to **Fern Grotto** (a natural amphitheater covered in ferns, reachable only by water) are offered *(see "What to Do," this chapter).*

Kaua'i Museum (4) *(4428 Rice St., Lihu'e, 808-245-6931, www.kauaimuseum.org, M–F 9AM–4PM, Sa 10AM–4PM, closed Su; free admission 1st Sa every month)* is housed in two of the most beautiful structures in old Lihu'e: the **A. S. Wilcox Memorial Building** and the modern **William Hyde Rice Building**. Changing exhibits acquaint visitors with the history of pre- and post-contact Kaua'i and Ni'ihau (the privately owned island across the channel, part of Kaua'i County), Captain Cook's arrival, and artifacts such as poi pounders, fishhooks, and *tapa* (cloth-making) implements, as well as artifacts from sugar plantations, Missionary furniture, pottery, photographs, books, art, saddles, and WWII memorabilia. Its **Edith King Wilcox Museum Gift Shop** *(808-246-2470)* is an excellent place to purchase Niʻihau-shell *leis*, native woods, ceramics, locally made bags, hats, books, and other gifts.

Built in 1935 by sugar baron Gaylord Wilcox, the plantation-style mansion on **Kilohana Plantation (5)** *(3-2087 Kaumualiʻi Hwy./Hwy. 50, Lihuʻe, 808-245-5608, www.kilohana kauai.com, 9:30AM–9:30PM)* was to be Kauaʻi's most expensive, most beautiful home. Now lovingly restored, the structure houses two levels of shops and galleries and **Gaylord's Restaurant ($$) (29)** *(see page 160)*. The 15,000 square foot mansion is set on 35 acres of grounds with tropical pleasure gardens, a working farm, and Kilohana Camp, a century-old workers' village. Visitors may stroll the plantation and shops, or take a Clydesdale-drawn carriage or "big red wagon" ride for a teatime tour in the afternoon. The vintage-style rail cars of the **Kauai Plantation Railway (15)** *(see page 158)*, pulled by a steam engine, provide another way to see the plantation grounds.

Kauai Aadheenam Monastery (6) *(107 Kaholalele Rd. off Kuamoʻo Rd., Wailua, 808-822-3012, www.himalayan academy.com/ssc/hawaii)* is a 458-acre Hindu sanctuary that comprises temples, statuary, botanical gardens, and ponds. You may take a self-guided tour of the front monastery area *(open daily 9AM–noon)*. A guided, 90-minute tour of the monastery is offered about once per week *(call 888-735-1619 for dates & reservations)*. Guests are requested to dress modestly. No T-shirts, shorts, short dresses, or tank tops. Polo-style shirts are OK.

Stroll picturesque **Kapaʻa (7)** *(Hwy. 56 north from Wailua; if road is congested, try bypass road on the left bet. mile markers 6 & 7)*; the quaint 19th-century coastal village's main street and short side streets are home to an array of specialty boutiques, cafés, and restaurants.

WHAT TO DO
Air Tours:
As much of Kauaʻi is inaccessible, ★**AIR TOURS** of its canyons, mountains, beaches, and waterfalls are very popular. The cowboys at **Island Helicopters (8)** *(heliport, Lihuʻe Airport, 808-245-8588 or 800-829-5999, www.island helicopters.com, hours vary by tour)* will give you the ride of your life. Or, for a different air tour altogether, try **Tropical Biplanes (9)** *(commuter terminal, Lihuʻe airport, 808-246-9123 or 888-280-9123, www. tropicalbiplanes.com, hours vary by tour)*, piloting Cessna 182 Skylane and WACO biplane tours. Customers rave about the open cockpit experience. The vintage-looking planes were actually built just a few years ago.

TOP PICK!

Beaches:

Protected **Kalapaki Beach (10)** *(behind Kauai Marriott Resort, Rice Rd., off Hwy. 56, Lihue, open daily)* is ideal for swimmers, novice surfers, and bodysurfers. You can also reach it through **Nawiliwili Park** *(behind Anchor*

Cove Shopping Ctr.). **Nawiliwili Bay** is the port of entry for cruise ships and the container ships that supply Kauaʻi with much of its goods. **Lydgate Beach Park (11)** *(Nalu Rd. off Hwy. 56, Wailua, www.kauaiexplorer.com/kauai_beaches/lydgate_beach_park.php, daily dawn–dusk)* is one of the most popular parks on Kauaʻi. It's attractive to swimmers, families (with an enclosed pond and playgrounds for kids), and picnickers. Lifeguards are on duty. Facilities include restrooms, showers, tables for picnicking, and bike paths.

Watersports:

Rent kayaks or join one of several guided tours upriver at **Wailua River Kayak Adventures (12)** *(6575 Kuamoʻo Rd., Kapaʻa, 808-822-5795 or 808-639-6332, http://kauaiwailuakayak.com, hours vary by tour).* They also lead hikes. **Smith's Fern Grotto Wailua River Cruise (13)** *(departs from Wailua Marina State Park, Wailua, 808-821-6895, www.smithskauai.com, 6 tours daily)* is just one of the activities offered by the enterprising Smith family *(see also page 161).* The two-hour trip on a canopied motor barge to natural wonder **Fern Grotto** and back includes songs, stories, and a hula lesson.

Golf:

Marriott Golf's **Kaua'i Lagoons Golf Club (14)** *(3351 Ho'olaulea Way, Lihu'e, 808-241-6000 or 800-634-6400, www.kauailagoonsgolf.com, call for tee times)* features two 40-acre-plus courses and 18 Jack Nicklaus Signature holes. Kaua'i Marriott Resort guests receive a discount on greens fees.

More Activities:

Kaua'i is famous for being Hollywood's idea of paradise, from *South Pacific* (much of it shot in Hanalei Bay) to Elvis Presley's *Blue Hawaii*, from *Gilligan's Island* to *Fantasy Island*,

from *Jurassic Park* to *Raiders of the Lost Ark*. Learn about Kaua'i-filmed movies and shows on **Hawaii Movie Tours (15)** *(4-885 Kuhio Hwy., Kapa'a, 808-822-1192 or 800-628-8432, www.hawaiimovietour.com, van tour daily, 4x4 tour M–F)*. Choose to ride in an air-conditioned van (with a TV monitor that allows you to watch scenes at the locations where they were filmed) or four-wheel-drive vehicle. The experience includes plenty of movie and TV lore, songs, and general frivolity. The tours also visit the site of the old **Coco Palms**, the legendary Polynesian-style resort run by visionary hotelier Grace Guslander. Grace's guests were greeted by doormen blowing conch shells and thrilled to the resort's evening torch lighting ceremonies (invented here). Elvis "married" Joan Blackman here in the movie *Blue Hawaii*. The resort's beautiful stand of palms was planted in

1896, and unlike the hotel, was not destroyed by Hurricane Iniki in 1992.

The Grayline company's **Polynesian Adventure Tours (16)** *(provides hotel pick up, office located at 4031 Halau St. #4, Lihu'e, 808-833-3000 or 800-622-3011, www.poly ad.com, tour hours vary)* offers two excursions on Kaua'i, and a one-day "fly-away" tour of the U.S.S. *Arizona* Memorial and Pearl Harbor on Oahu island, leaving from Lihu'e Airport.

Especially popular with guests of the Kilohana Plantation (5) *(see page 154)* is a train/hike/lunch/orchard tour or a *lu'au*/train tour with the steam-powered **Kaua'i Plantation Railway (17)** *(Kiholana Plantation, 808-245-RAIL or 7245, www.kauaiplantationrailway.com)*. A 40-minute train ride around the plantation is also offered five times a day, and a late-afternoon ride is added Tuesdays and Fridays.

Visit a chocolate orchard (and a vanilla grove and bamboo forest), learn about the cacao tree and how its fruit becomes chocolate, then enjoy an 11-course dark chocolate tasting. It's all part of the three-hour "From Branch to Bar" chocolate tour at **Steelgrass Farm (18)** *(Kapa'a, specific directions provided after reservations are made, 808-821-1857, www.steelgrass.org/chocolate, tours M, W, F 9AM)*.

PLACES TO EAT & DRINK

Two local places offer outstanding food at great prices: Unassuming but award-winning **Hamura Saimin Stand**

(19) ($) *(2956 Kress St., Lihu'e, 808-245-3271, M–Th 10AM–11PM, F–Sa 10AM–midnight, Su 10AM–9:30PM)* attracts droves of locals and visitors for bowls of noodle soup and amazing *liliko'i* (passion fruit) pie. The similarly no frills décor at mainstay **Barbecue Inn (20) ($)** *(2982 Kress St., Lihu'e, 808-245-2921, serving breakfast, lunch, & dinner M–Sa)* doesn't detract from a flavorful Hawaiian/American/Asian menu. Tempura, prime rib, scampi, and more are served with soup and salad. Prices are easy on the wallet so eat hearty, but save room for dessert; the pie karma is excellent here, too. Tasty take-out plate lunches and seafood platters from **The Fish Express (21) ($)** *(3-3343 Kuhio Hwy./Hwy. 56, Lihu'e, 808-245-9918, M–Sa 10AM–6PM, Su 10AM–4PM)* are perfect for impromptu picnics. Fresh and frozen seafood available, too. **Hanalima Baking (22) ($)** *(4495 Puhi Rd., Lihu'e, 808-246-8816, www.geocities.com/bake_kauai, M–F 6AM–12:30PM, Sa 7AM–12:30PM)* offers just-baked cookies, breads, and pastries from original recipes, plus coffee and quick breakfasts to go. Check out the taro breads and crab rolls. Go early for best selection.

The parking lot at **Kintaro (23) ($-$$)** *(4-370 Kuhio Hwy./Hwy. 56, Kapa'a, 808-822-3341, serving dinner M–Sa)* is always crowded, and with good reason. The Japanese fare here is authentic, attractive, and delicious. Fresh sushi, traditional dishes, and serene décor make this a top pick. **Hukilau Lanai (24) ($-$$)** *(Kauai Coast Resort, behind Coconut MarketPlace, 520 Aleka Loop, Kapa'a, 808-822-0600, Tu–Su 5PM–10PM)* is a favorite with locals and visitors for its open-air, torch-lit ambiance, tasty *pupus*, and live entertainment *(Su, Tu, F)*. Get that plate lunch fix at **Aloha Diner (25) ($)** *(971 Kuhio Hwy./Hwy. 56, #F, Kapa'a, 808-822-3851, Tu–Sa 10:30AM–2:30PM & 5:30PM–8:30PM)*. Big plates, little prices. For a fresh spin on plate lunches, wraps, and burritos, try **Mermaids Café (26) ($)** *(4-1384 Kuhio Hwy./Hwy. 56, Kapa'a, 808-821-2026, daily 11AM–9PM)*. There's a walk-up window and a few tables on the street, so you can sit outside and sip your hibiscus lemonade.

Among Kaua'i's most lauded restaurants, **Blossoming Lotus (27) ($)** *(4504 Kukui St., Kapa'a, 808-822-7678, www.blossominglotus.com, daily 5PM–9PM, Su brunch 10AM–2PM)* raises the bar for vegan cuisine with a menu that includes such dishes as "Pan's Seared Pink-Oyster Mushroom Salad" and "Ulysses' Udon Odyssey." Its **Lotus Root Juice Bar (28) ($)** *(4-1384 Kuhio Hwy./Hwy. 56, 808-823-6658, daily 7AM–6PM)* serves pastries, "ice crème," and smoothies.

At Kilohana Plantation (5), **Gaylord's Restaurant (29) ($$)** *(3-2087 Kaumuali'i Hwy., Lihu'e, 808-245-9593, http://gaylordskauai.com, serving breakfast, lunch, & dinner daily, brunch on Su)* offers a varied menu. Seafood, lamb, and venison are among its signature entrées; other dishes feature ingredients grown on the plantation.

Bars, Nightlife, & *Lu'uas*:

Set in the old Kuboyama Hotel building, **Nawiliwili Tavern (30) ($)** *(3488 Paena Loop, Lihu'e, 808-245-1781, daily 2PM–2AM)* is a laid-back hangout with dancing, pool, darts, video games, TV sports, and karaoke nights. Locals and visitors like the easygoing atmosphere, pub food, and drinks. Kaua'i's gay community gathers here the first Saturday of each month.

The island's *pau hana* (after work) crowd packs the **Hula Girl Bar and Grill (31) ($-$$)** *(Coconut MarketPlace, 4-484 Kuhio Hwy./Hwy.56, Kapa'a, 808-822-4422, www.kauaimenu.com/MenuPages/KauaiHulaGirl/hulagirl.htm, serving lunch & dinner daily)* for happy hour mai tais, music, and vibe. Evening diners enjoy live music at **Blossoming Lotus (27)**; on Saturdays, they stay for sakitinis, dance parties, and DJs at its **Lotus Lounge (32)** *(4504 Kukui St., Kapa'a, call for schedule updates, 808-822-7678, www.blossominglotus.com, Sa 10PM–2AM)*. **Pizzetta (33) ($-$$)** *(1387 Kuhio Hwy./Hwy. 56, Kapa'a, 808-823-8882, www.pizzetarestaurant.com, daily 11AM–9:30PM)* serves up pasta, salads, pizza, calzones, and paninis, accompanied by live music and DJs on weekends *(F–Sa 10PM–1:30PM)*.

An entertainment extravaganza, the popular **Smith Family Garden Lu'au (34) ($$$)** *(Smith's Tropical Paradise,*

Wailua Marina State Park, 174 Wailua Rd., Wailua, 808-821-6895, www.smithskauai.com, M, W, F 5PM) features *imu*-roasted pig, a bountiful buffet, and the music and dance of Hawaii, Tahiti, and Samoa.

WHERE TO SHOP

Kukui Grove Shopping Center (35) *(3-2600 Kaumuali'i Hwy./Hwy. 50, Lihu'e, 808-246-9583, www.kukuigrovecenter.com, M–Th 9:30AM–7PM, F to 9PM, Sa to 7PM, Su 10AM–6PM)* is the big mall on Kaua'i, with Macy's, K-Mart, and Sears anchoring smaller specialty shops and eateries,

including Jamba Juice and Starbucks. Be sure to check out **Kauai Products Store** *(808-246-67530, www.kauai productsstore.com)*, selling locally produced koa wood clocks and bowls, pottery, clothing, coffee, chocolate, and gifts. Fresh, locally grown produce, flowers, and Kaua'i-made products are available at Sunshine Market (36) *(Vidinha Stadium, Ho'olako Rd., Lihu'e, 808-742-1834, www.kauai.gov, F 3PM)*, Kukui Grove Center Monday Market (37) *(3-2600 Kaumuali'i Hwy./Hwy. 50, Lihu'e, 808-246-9583, www.kukuigrovecenter.com, M 3PM)*, and Kapa'a Sunshine Market (38) *(Kapa'a New Town Park, Kahau St., Kapa'a, 808-822-5887, www. kauai.gov, W 3PM)*. One of my favorite shops on Kaua'i is the Stitchery (39) *(3-3551 Kuhio Hwy., Lihu'e, 808-245-2281, M–Sa 9AM–5PM)*. This is the best place to find sewing supplies and quality fabrics that stand up to tropical weather and come out looking fresh. Japanese cottons and Balinese prints are stacked alongside displays of ready-made garments, quilts, and other items created by local seamstresses, all at reasonable prices.

Coconut MarketPlace (40) *(484 Kuhio Hwy., Kapaʻa, 808-822-3641, www.coconutmarketplace.com, M–Sa 9AM–9PM, Su 10AM–6PM)* features more than 60 shops and restaurants. Weekly hula shows, a farmer's market, and sidewalk days with live entertainment make up the calendar. The mall is near the old **Coco Palms** resort site *(see page 157)*. Craftspeople, souvenir vendors, seamstresses, farmers, wellness practitioners, and others pack the Kauaʻi Products Fair (41) *(Kuhio Hwy., northern Kapaʻa, 808-246-0988, Th–Su 9AM–5PM)*, on the *mauka* or mountain side of the road. Go for pearls and jewelry, quilts, handmade stationery items, sand-stuffed animals, Hawaiian music, a massage, and much more.

WHERE TO STAY

Well-located Kaha Lani Resort (42) ($$) *(4460 Nehe Rd., Lihuʻe, 808-822-9331 or 800-367-5004, www.castleresorts.com/Home/accommodations/kaha-lani-resort)* is convenient to activities all over the island. Stay in a spacious one- or two-bedroom condo with kitchen and cable TV. Guests may access the resort's putting green, tennis court, pool, barbeques, and washers/dryers. As with all privately owned condos, specify what you want before you book. Check the resort's Web site for online specials. Kauai Coast Resort at

the Beachboy (43) ($$) *(520 Aleka Loop, Kapaʻa, 808-822-3441 or 866-729-7182, www.shellhospitality.com/hotels/kauai_coast_resort)* is behind the Coconut MarketPlace (41); it offers updated studios (compact refrigerator, microwave, and coffeemaker) and one- and two-bedroom condos (kitchen with refrigerator, range, dishwasher, and washer/dryer). All come with private *lanais* with garden or ocean views, cable TV, pool/Jacuzzi, and restaurant.

Rosewood Kauaʻi Vacation Rentals (44) ($-$$) *(872 Kamalu Rd., Kapaʻa, 808-822-5216, www.rosewoodkauai.com)* handles rental properties in a range of prices, mostly in the Wailua/Coconut Coast area. Offerings include country homes, beach homes and cottages, condos, apartments, and a backpacker hostel.

A bit off the beaten path, Kauaʻi Inn (45) ($) *(2430 Hulemalu Rd., Lihuʻe, 808-245-9000 or 800-808-2330, www.kauai-inn.com)* is a pleasant, 48-room hotel on the edge of a residential neighborhood. Rooms surround a courtyard and pool, where coffee and pastries are served each morning. Amenities include ceiling fans, microwaves, refrigerators, Internet access, and private baths. Air conditioning is extra.

If all you want is a very basic room (linoleum floors, no phone), the Tip Top Motel (46) ($) *(3173 Akahi St., Lihuʻe, 808-245-2333)* might do. A block from Kuhio Hwy./Hwy.56, it faces a residential street. Its **Tip Top Café**

($) (open for breakfast & lunch, closed M) is known for bargain-priced breakfasts (try the pancakes). Check in at the restaurant/lobby.

Kauai International Hostel (47) ($) *(4532 Lehua St., Kapa'a, 808-823-6142, www.kauaihostel.net)* offers affordable accommodations. Dorm-style bunks start at $25 *(walk-ins $30, if available)*; private rooms run $60 and up. Bring your own soap, shampoo, and towels. Lights out at 11PM.

Hula is ... the heartbeat of the Hawaiian people.

David Kalakaua,
King of Hawaii, 1874-1891

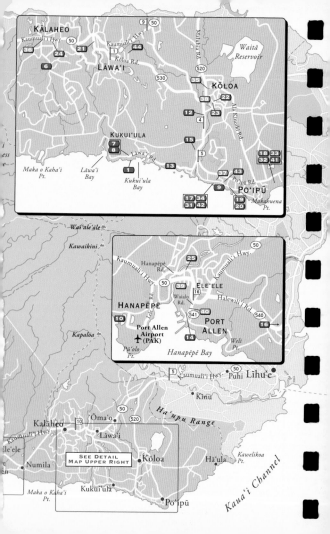

SOUTH & WEST KAUA'I

5 Mile marker

0 ————— 4 miles
0 ————— 4 km

N

Na Pali Coast State Park

Kalalau Foot Trail

Hono'onāpali Natural Area Reserve

5 30

Keawanui Landing

Mākaha Pt.

Ku'ia Natural Area Reserve

4 *Kōke'e State Park*

Ala Wilde Pres

Polihale State Park

2

Nohili Pt.

Na Pali- Kona Forest Reserve

Kōke'e Rd.

Waimea Canyon State Park

Waimea Canyon

550

3

Kao Rd. • Mānā

Barking Sands Airfield

Mānā Rd.

Kōke'e Rd.

550

Waimea Cyn. Dr.

Waimea R.

Kaumuali'i Hwy.

Kokole Pt.

11 • Kekaha

552

SEE DETAIL MAP BELOW LEFT

50

25

• Waimea

Kāpalawai •

Pākala • • Ka'awanui

50

Hanapēpē Heights

Olokele • Kaumakani •

Hanapēpē

Port Allen Airport (PAK)

Pa'aka Pt.

SEE DETAIL MAP ABOVE

29 26

550

50

Waimea Cyn. Dr.

45

WAIMEA

Kaumuali'i Hwy.

Menehune Rd.

27 23

28

46

Waimea R.

50

chapter 9

SOUTH & WEST KAUA'I

SOUTH & WEST KAUA'I

What to See:

1. Spouting Horn
2. Polihale State Park
3. WAIMEA CANYON STATE PARK ★
4. Koke'e State Park
5. Koke'e Natural History Museum
6. Kukuiolono Park and Golf Course
7. McBryde Gardens
8. Allerton Gardens

What to Do:

9. Po'ipu Beach County Park
10. Salt Pond Beach County Park
11. Kekaha Beach Park
12. Snorkel Bob's
13. Snuba Tours of Kaua'i
14. Kauai Sea Tours
15. Outfitters Kaua'i
16. Kaua'i Coffee Company

Places to Eat & Drink:

17. Naniwa Japanese Restaurant & Sushi Bar
18. Tidepools
19. Brennecke's Beach Broiler
20. Brennecke's Beach Deli
21. Pizzetta
22. Koloa Fish Market
23. Sueoka's Snack Shop
24. Kalaheo Café & Coffee Company
25. Hanapepe Café & Espresso
26. Shrimp Station
27. Jo-Jo's Shave Ice
28. Jo-Jo's Anuenue Shave Ice & Treats
29. Waimea Brewing Company
30. Lodge at Koke'e
31. The Point
32. Stevenson's Library
33. Grand Hyatt Kauai Lu'au
34. Surf to Sunset Luau

Where to Shop:

35. Sunshine Market Koloa
36. Sunshine Market Kalaheo
37. Po'ipu Shopping Village
38. Old Koloa Town
39. Hanapepe
40. Kauai Chocolate Company

★ *Top Picks*

Where to Stay:

Kaua'i's original name is
Kaua'i-a-mamo-ka-la-ni-po,
"the fountain head of many waters
from on high and bubbling
up from below."

SOUTH & WEST KAUA'I

• SNAPSHOT •

Welcome to the Garden Isle! Kaua'i's nickname is reinforced by its zoning ordinances. Less than five percent of the island's land may be developed, and no building may be taller than a mature coconut palm tree, about 40 feet. Most of this developed land is situated on the coastal plains ringing the island. South Kaua'i, especially around the Po'ipu beaches, is home to many of the island's posher resorts, complete with fantasy settings and elaborate spas. Both traffic and people thin out heading west. As the main road skirts the coastline to the mountainous section of the island, scenic villages and harbor towns give way to red dirt ravines and welcoming, white sand beaches. Some are calm, protected coves; others are wild and windy. Monitor conditions before you swim, and remember the Kaua'i saying: "No locals in the water—don't go out."

Turn north at Waimea or Kekaha to discover what Mark Twain called the "Grand Canyon of the Pacific"—spectacular Waimea Canyon State Park, bordered on the north by the isolated Na Pali Coast. Continue west on Kaumuali'i Highway/Highway 50 to the Barking Sands Naval Facility. The facility is closed to visitors, but access is allowed to one of Kaua'i's most popular beaches: Polihale State Park Beach.

The island of Ni'ihau, visible across the Kaulakahi Channel, is part of Kaua'i but has been privately owned since 1864. Today it's off limits to all except the owner's family, U.S. Navy personnel, government officials, and invited guests. Ni'ihau is famous for its tiny shells, each no bigger than a grain of rice. Necklaces made from them may fetch thousands of dollars from collectors.

WHAT TO SEE

Seeing the sun set behind the Spouting Horn (1) *(Spouting Horn Beach Pk., Koloa, open daily)* is one of those touristy things you just have to do. The natural wonder is caused by massive waves that force seawater to rush up and out through the end of a lava tube. An adjoining blowhole channels air, creating dramatic moaning sounds said to be those of a legendary giant *mo'o*, or lizard.

The locals' favorite South Kaua'i beach is Polihale State Park (2) *(end of 4-mile dirt road from Mana village, off Kaumuali'i Hwy./Hwy. 50, www.hawaiistateparks.org/parks/kauai, daily dawn–dusk)*. Those who endure the long drive over the rutted, unpaved road to get here are rewarded by a scenic beach with dunes and views of the stunning Na Pali sea cliffs. Sunsets and the star-filled nights are dazzling. This is a wild beach: you may surf and swim in summer if conditions are calm, but beware strong currents year round. It can be extra hot and sunny. Showers, toilets, picnic tables, barbecue pits, and drinking water are available.

★WAIMEA CANYON STATE PARK (3) *(Koke'e Rd., Waimea, www.hawaiistateparks.org/parks/kauai, daily dawn–dusk)* is spectacular. The dramatic cliffs and steep ravines that form the canyons seem almost too grand for such a small island, but that makes the unusual formations extra special. The walls of the canyons are striated with peach, red, gray, and other

hues that glow in late afternoon sunlight. Long-tailed white tropicbirds soar hundreds of feet below to unreachable nests. Every overlook demands a stop. Hiking is available at several pullouts along the road and biking down from the summit is a popular pastime *(see "What to Do," this chapter).*

Koke'e State Park (4) *(Koke'e Rd., Waimea, www.hawaiistateparks.org/parks/kauai, daily dawn–dusk)* is literally the end of the road. One overlook provides commanding views of the steep-sided Kalalau Valley from 4,000 feet above the valley floor. Hiking in forest reserves and along the Waimea Canyon rim is popular here. The weather is often cool and damp; be prepared. The park's **Koke'e Natural History Museum (5)** *(3600 Koke'e Rd., 808-335-9975, www.kokee.org, daily 9AM–4PM)* has hiking maps and information on native birds, plants, and animals.

Kukuiolono Park & Golf Course (6) *(off Hwy. 50, follow signs, 808-332-9151, park open daily 7AM-6:30 PM)* offers visitors stunning views of the mountains and sea,

Japanese gardens, and a collection of stones said to have been placed here by the mythical *Menehune*.

The **National Tropical Botanical Gardens** *(Visitors Center, 4425 Lawa'i Rd., Lawa'i, 808-742-2623, www. ntbg.org, daily 8:30AM–5PM)* oversees two adjacent properties on the south side of Kaua'i and another on the north end (in addition to a garden in Maui and one in Florida). The gardens are dedicated to botanical and horticultural research and the preservation of endangered tropical plants. The organization's largest property on the south side, **McBryde Gardens (7)** *(808-742-2623, self-guided tours daily & a guided tour Su 9AM; reach the garden via tram from the 4425 Lawa'i Rd. Visitors Center)* is a living laboratory of exotic, rare, and endangered plants; the site also features a Canoe Garden. **Allerton Gardens (8)** *(808-742-2623, guided tours given daily, reservations required, reach the garden via tram from the 4425 Lawa'i Rd. Visitors Center)* is more formal, with statuary, pools, and classical plantings.

WHAT TO DO
Beaches:
Popular **Po'ipu Beach County Park (9)** *(Hoowili Rd., Po'ipo, 808-241-4460, www.kauai.gov, open daily)* anchors the Po'ipu beaches. The park has picnic pavilions, comfort stations, and lifeguards. On its east end, **Brennecke Beach** attracts boogie boarders and body-surfers; farther west, **Lawa'i Beach** is a favorite of snorkelers. The protected cove at **Salt Pond Beach County Park (10)** *(Hwy. 50 past mile marker 17, 808-*

241-4460, www.kauai.gov, open daily) offers safe, easy swimming. The park has showers, comfort stations, a picnic area, shade, and lifeguards. Its natural salt pond has been used by natives for centuries to make sea salt. Note: Do not enter the salt-making area without permission. Picnic tables and restrooms make **Kekaha Beach Park (11)** (*Hwy. 50, bet. mile markers 26 & 27, open daily*) a great place for a break, and snorkeling and swimming are good when the water is calm. Use caution. This long, sandy beach is one of the best places around to see expert wind- and kite-surfers.

Watersports:

Snorkel Bob's (12) (*3236 Po'ipu Rd., Koloa, 808-742-2206, http://snorkelbob.com, daily 8AM–5PM*) is everywhere. Take advantage of their snorkel and boogie board specials. Snuba may be a new concept to some, but **Snuba Tours of Kaua'i (13)** (*1604 Papau Pl., Kapa'a, snuba location: sandy shores of Lawa'i Beach near Po'ipui, 808-823-8912, www.snubakauai.com, M–F 9AM, 10:30AM, noon, 1:30PM*) makes it easy: in a cross between snorkeling and scuba diving, participants are tethered to a 20-foot-long line that allows them to dive lower in the water and breathe from tanks on surface rafts. Enjoy a day of snorkeling and lunch on a distant beach with **Kauai Sea Tours (14)** (*Port Allen Marina Center, 4353 Waialo Rd., Ste. 2B-3B, 'Ele'ele, 808-826-PALI or 800-733-7997, www.kauaiseatours.com, tour hours vary*). Their well-appointed 60-foot *Lucky Lady* catamaran and thrilling rigid-hulled rafts allow you to explore the inaccessible Na Pali coast.

More Activities:
Outfitters Kauai (15) *(2827-A Po'ipu Rd., Po'ipu, 808-742-9667, www.outfitterskauai. com, tour days & hours vary)* rents bikes and leads tours to explore Waimea Canyon. This eco-minded company also

guides visitors on kayak tours, hikes, and zipline tours, and it offers trips that include all these activities. The company has access to private areas (such as the Kipu Ranch), making for exclusive adventure. One tour offers visitors an opportunity to unleash their inner Tarzans and Janes by swinging out on a rope and dropping 20 feet into a black-water pool.

The Visitor Center at **Kaua'i Coffee Company (16)** *(1 Numila Rd., 'Ele'ele, off Hwy. 50, 808-335-5497, www. kauaicoffee.com, daily 9AM–5PM)* acquaints caffeine addicts and others with the process of growing, harvesting, and processing coffee. A self-guided walking tour takes you around the plantation. Samples are available for tasting. The gift shop sells beans, ground coffee, and island souvenirs.

PLACES TO EAT & DRINK
Where to Eat:
The resorts in the Po'ipu area all offer top-quality restaurant experiences. A couple of standouts: **Naniwa Japanese Restaurant & Sushi Bar (17) ($$-$$$)** *(Sheraton Kaua'i Resort, 2440 Ho'onani Rd., Koloa, 808-742-*

4011, *www.sheraton-kauai.com, Sa 5:30PM–9:30PM*), for its sushi, and **Tidepools (18) ($$-$$$)** (*Grand Hyatt Kauai Resort & Spa, 1571 Po'ipu Rd., Koloa, www.kauai.hyatt.com, 808-240-6456, daily 5:30PM–10PM*), for its contemporary Hawaiian cuisine served in open-air thatched huts with waterfalls and koi-filled lagoons. Reservations recommended for both restaurants.

Brennecke's Beach Broiler (19) ($-$$) (*2100 Ho'one Rd., Po'ipu Beach, Koloa, 808-742-7588, www.brenneckes.com, daily 11AM–10PM*) serves lunch and dinner in a pleasant open-air, second-floor setting across from Brennecke Beach. The menu includes fresh fish and beef entrées, plus burgers, salads, and sandwiches. Reservations recommended. Downstairs, **Brennecke's Beach Deli (20) ($)** (*808-742-7588, www.brenneckes.com/deli.html, daily 11AM–10PM*) sells "picnic packages," cold beer, sandwiches, shave ice, coffee, ice cream, batteries, and more.

Pizzetta (21) ($) (*5408 Koloa Rd., Koloa, 808-742-8881, www.pizzettarestaurant.com, M–F 11AM–9PM, Sa-Su 11AM–10PM*) serves crispy pizzas, pasta dishes, and fresh salads. Their Kapa'a branch has late-night entertainment (*see page 161*). You'll find the freshest fish, island-style, and good plate lunches at the down-home **Koloa Fish Market (22) ($)** (*5482 Koloa Rd., Koloa, 808-742-6199, M–Sa 10AM–5PM*), next to the Big Save market. **Sueoka's Snack Shop (23) ($)** (*5392 Koloa Rd., Koloa, 808-742-11121, Tu-Sa 9AM–2:30PM, cash only*), the fast-food arm of the next-door grocery store, dishes up great fish sandwiches and plate lunches at low prices.

Kalaheo Café & Coffee Company (24) ($-$$) *(2-2560 Kaumuali'i Hwy./Hwy. 50, Kalaheo, 808-332-5858, www.kalaheo.com, M–Sa 6:30AM–2:30PM, Su 6:30AM– 2PM, W–Sa 5:30PM–10PM)* serves hearty breakfasts, soups, salads, and sandwiches. They also sell made-on-the-premises baked goods and Hawaiian coffees by the cup and pound. Look for the sign with the sun on the *makai* (ocean) side of the road.

Among the best places to eat in the area, **Hanapepe Café & Espresso (25) ($)** *(3830 Hanapepe Rd., Hanapepe, 808-335-5011, M–Th 7AM–2PM, F 6AM–9PM)* is known for its vegetarian and seafood entrées.

Roadside stand **Shrimp Station (26) ($)** *(9652 Kaumuali'i Hwy./Hwy. 50, Waimea, 808-338-1242, www.shrimp station.com, daily 11AM–8PM)* sells, well, shrimp— baked, boiled, breaded, fried—with accompaniments. Coconut shrimp is a favorite.

Shave ice enthusiasts have a running debate over which Waimea spot is best—**Jo-Jo's Shave Ice (27) ($)** *(19-835 Kaumuali'i Hwy./Hwy. 50, Waimea, 808-635-7615, daily 11AM–5PM)* or the myriad flavors of **Jo-Jo's Anuenue Shave Ice & Treats (28) ($)** *(5 Pokole Rd., Waimea, daily 10:30AM–6PM)* (*anuenue* means "rainbow") around the corner. Why not try both?

Worth a stop on the way to or from Waimea Canyon: **Waimea Brewing Company (29) ($)** *(Waimea Plantation Cottages, 9400 Kaumuali'i Hwy./Hwy. 50, Waimea, 808-338-1625, www.waimeaplantation.com/dining.php, daily*

11AM–9PM), with hand-crafted brews on tap and good pub food. Expect creative ethnic-influenced dishes, fresh fish, and crisp salads. The spot features live Hawaiian or bluegrass music some nights. The **Lodge at Koke'e (30) ($)** *(3600 Koke'e Rd., Waimea, 808-335-6061, www. kokeelodgekauai.com, daily 9AM–5PM)* provides basic breakfasts, salads, sandwiches, and local favorites for hungry campers and hikers.

Bars, Nightlife, & *Lu'aus*:

The Point (31) *(Sheraton, 2440 Ho'onani Rd., Koloa, 808-742-1661, www.sheraton-kauai.com/de_thepoint.htm, daily 11AM–midnight)* is a sleek, modern bar that affords great views of the ocean and the hotel's torch-lighting ceremony and Hawaiian show. Live entertainment is featured *(Th 8:30PM–11:30PM, F & Sa 9:30PM–12:30AM)*. Leave the wet bathing suit and flip-flops behind before entering elegant **Stevenson's Library (32)** *(Grand Hyatt Kauai Resort & Spa, 1571 Poipu Rd., Koloa, www.kauai.hyatt.com, nightly 6PM–midnight)*, with its bookcases, billiard tables, backgammon, and chess sets. Enjoy live jazz *(8PM–11PM)*. *Pupus* offered nightly, sushi over the weekends *(F–M 6PM–9PM)*.

The **Grand Hyatt Kauai Luau (33) ($$$$)** *(Grand Hyatt Kauai Resort & Spa, 1571 Po'ipu Rd., Koloa, www.kauai. hyatt.com, 808-240-6456, Su & Th 6PM–8:30PM)* includes a *lei* greeting, buffet, open bar, hula lessons, and Hawaiian crafts. Reservations recommended. The Sheraton's **Surf to Sunset Luau (34) ($$$$)** *(Sheraton Kauai Resort, 2440 Ho'onani Rd., Koloa, 808-742-8205,* *www.sheraton-kauai.com/de_skluau.htm, M & F check-in 5PM)* is Kaua'i's only oceanfront *lu'au*. It also offers an extensive menu of traditional and ethnic-inspired dishes, accompanied by award-winning entertainment. Reservations recommended.

WHERE TO SHOP

Sunshine Markets bring farmers and buyers together. Try either Sunshine Market Koloa (35) *(Koloa Ball Pk., Maluhia Rd., Koloa, M noon)* or Sunshine Market Kalaheo (36) *(Kalaheo Neighborhood Ctr., 4480 Papalina Rd. off Kaumauli'i Hwy./Hwy. 50, 808-332-9770, Tu 3PM)*.

Po'ipu Shopping Village (37) *(2360 Kiahuna Plantation Dr., Koloa, 808-742-2831, www.poipubeach.org, M–Sa 9:30AM–9PM, Su 10AM–7PM)* offers more than 50 shops, services, and eateries, from gifts to groceries, as well as Tahitian dance, fire knife dancing, and drumming shows.

You'll drive through the **Tree Tunnel** *(Maluhia Rd.)*, a grove of eucalyptus trees planted in the 1800s, on your way to colorful Old Koloa Town (38) *(off Maluhia Rd./Rte.520 from Kaumauli'i Hwy./Hwy. 50, Koloa, www.oldkoloa.com)*, Hawaii's first sugar plantation town. Shops include **Island Soap & Candle Works** *(Old Koloa Town Shopping Ctr., Koloa, 808-742-1945, www. kauaisoap.com, daily 9AM–10PM)*, purveyors of fragrant handmade soaps and candles, and **Sueoka's** *(5392 Koloa Rd., Koloa, 808-742-1112, M–Sa 7AM–9PM)*, an old-fashioned grocery store that's been around since 1916.

Hanapepe (39) *(off Kaumuali'i Hwy./Hwy. 50)*, Kaua'i's "Biggest Little Town," is home to several art galleries, among them **Banana Patch Studio** *(3685 Hanapepe Rd., 808-335-5944, http://bananapatchstudio.com, M–Th 10AM–4:30PM, F 10AM–9PM, Sa 10AM–4PM)*, featuring ceramic tiles and pottery. The town hosts an Art Night every Friday *(808-335-0343, 6PM–9PM)*. Galleries open, musicians play, and **Hanapepe Café & Espresso (25)** stays open. While you're here, check out the rope footbridge that spans the Hanapepe River.

Kaua'i Chocolate Company (40) *(Port Allen Marina Center, 4341 Waiola Rd., 'Ele'ele, 808-335-0448, www.kauai chocolate.us, M–Sa 11AM– 5PM)*, features locally-grown goodness. Specialties include chocolate *'opihis* (limpets) made of shortbread cookie, caramel, and macadamia nut, covered in chocolate. This writer's favorite: "Da Brick," layered toffee, caramel, and chocolate.

WHERE TO STAY
Grand Hyatt Kauai Resort and Spa (41) ($$$$) *(1571 Po'ipu Rd., Koloa, 808-742-1234, http://kauai.hyatt. com/hyatt/hotels/index.jsp)* is a tropical fantasy. Pools (with a 150-foot water slide and waterfalls), saltwater lagoon, beach, and the adjacent Robert Trent Jones Po'ipu Bay Golf Course offer relaxation and recreation. The island décor and landscaping of the private *hales* at Anara Spa delight the eye, while services spoil the sybarite within. This resort is lessening its environmental impact with the installation of a solar-power system designed to replace a portion of its energy needs.

Community supporter **Sheraton Kauai Resort (42) ($$$-$$$$$)** *(2440 Ho'onani Rd., Koloa, 808-742-1661, www.sheratonkauai.com)* offers guests a chance to *malama Kaua'i* (take care of Kaua'i) by opting for a special package that enables you to volunteer on environmental and cultural projects. This comfortable hotel boasts good restaurants, a popular lounge, and a beautiful setting.

Next to the Sheraton (you can see its *lu'au* from the beach), **Kiahuna Plantation & The Beach Bungalows (43) ($$-$$$$)** *(2253B Po'ipu Rd., Koloa, 808-742-2200 or 800-367-5004, www.castleresorts.com)* is a condominium resort offering individually-owned, one- and two-bedroom properties on 35 landscaped acres. Garden view, partial ocean view, and sea view units vary in updates and furnishings—confirm details ahead of time. **Po'ipu Shopping Village (37)**, with boutiques and eateries, is across the street.

High above the sea in the cool uplands between Kalaheo and Koloa, the **Kauai Banyan Inn (44) ($$)** *(3528B Mana Hema Pl., Koloa, 808-742-7525 or 888-786-3855, www.kauaibanyan.com/koa.htm)* has all the comforts for reasonable prices. Five rooms and a cottage are available. Get exact directions, as finding the inn is tricky the first time.

The one- to four-bedroom guesthouses of award-winning **Waimea Plantation Cottages (45) ($$$-$$$$)** *(9400 Kaumuali'i Hwy./Hwy. 50, Waimea, 808-338-1625, 877-997-6667, www.waimeaplantation.com)* are restored historic cottages with kitchens and *lanais* set in a coconut grove. Visitors may also opt for off-site estate houses (three- and five-bedroom). Each structure comes with period furnishings. Take a walking tour of the cottages *(808-335-2824, Tu, Th, Sa)*. Be pampered at the **Hideaway Spa** on-site.

Inn Waimea (46) ($-$$) *(4469 Halepule Rd., Waimea, 808-338-0031, www.innwaimea.com)* offers four suites in a charming Craftsman-style home near the beach and business district. Rooms include phone, bath, cable TV, ceiling fan, refrigerator, coffeemaker, Internet, and private parking. The innkeepers also rent **cottages ($$)** in town.

The **Lodge at Koke'e (30) ($)** *(P.O. Box 367, Waimea, HI 96796, 808-355-6061, www.thelodgeatkokee.net)* offers no-frills cabins with wood-burning stoves, basic kitchens, and hot showers at the "Grand Canyon of the Pacific." The cabins are popular; book at least six months in advance. The lodge also has a restaurant *(see page 177)*.

Camping: **Polihale State Park (2)** *(see page 170)* has minimally developed tent sites. **Koke'e State Park (4)** *(see page 171)* offers tent camping spaces. To inquire about availability and make reservations at **Kaua'i State Parks**, contact the Division of State Parks *(808-587-0300, M–F, 8AM–3:30PM Hawaiian time, www.hawaiistateparks.org/camping/fees.cfm)* or reserve through the State Parks' Kaua'i District Office *(3060 Eiwa St., Rm. 306, Lihu'e, Hawaii 96766, 808-274-3444)*.

EFT

Kaweonui Pt.

Kalihiwai Bay

Kepuhi Pt.

8

● Princeville

Kalihiwai

56

Kilauea

● Kīlauea

6

1

560

✈ Princeville Airport (HDV)

Opaeka Rd.

Kalihiwai Rd.

56

Hanalei N.W.R.

18

Kuawa Rd.

Kūhiō Hwy.

16

l e a

Moloa'a Forest Reserve

e s e r v e

Kekōiki

Keālia Forest Reserve

SEE DETAIL MAP BELOW RIGHT

Moku 'ae'ae

Kīlauea Point Lighthouse ■

7

Kīlauea Point National Wildlfe Refuge

Mōkōlea Point

Lihu'e-Koloa Forest Reserve

Kauapea Beach

Makana'ano Pl.

Kīlauea Bay

Kīlauea Rd.

Secret Beach Rd.

Kīlauea R.

20
21
31

29

KĪLAUEA

6

Kalihiwai Rd.

Keneke St.

Kūhiō Hwy.

Oka St.

Kīlauea Falls

Wailapa Rd.

39

Liliukalani St.

22

23

Kolo Rd.

Kūhiō Hwy.

56

56

NORTH KAUAʻI

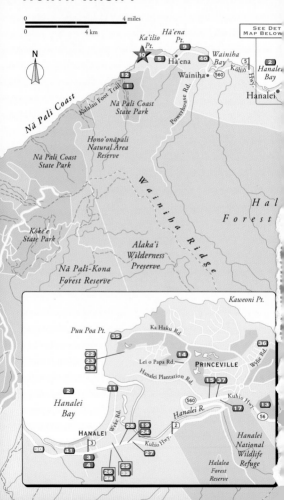

0 ——————— 4 miles
0 ——————— 4 km

N

Kaʻilio Pt.
Ka'ilio Pt. ★ 10
Hāʻena Pt.
9
5 Ha'ena
40
Wainiha Bay
Wainiha
560
Kūhiō Hwy.
5
2
Hanalei Bay
Hanalei

SEE DET
MAP BELOW

12
1

Kalalau Foot Trail

Nā Pali Coast
State Park

Nā Pali Coast

Hono'onāpali
Natural Area
Reserve

Powerhouse Rd.

Wainiha Ridge

Nā Pali Coast
State Park

Kōkeʻe
State Park

Hal
Forest

Alakaʻi
Wilderness
Preserve

Nā Pali-Kona
Forest Reserve

Kaweoni Pt.

Puu Poa Pt.

35

Ka Haku Rd.

36

22
23
25
38

14

Lei o Papa Rd.

PRINCEVILLE

Wjie Rd.

2

Hanalei Plantation Rd.

560

15
37

Kūhiō Hwy.

11

Hanalei Bay

Hanalei R.

17

13

56

28 19
24

2

Weke Rd.

HANALEI

3

Kūhiō Hwy.

27

Hanalei
National
Wildlife
Refuge

30

41

3
4

26
39

25
39

Halalea
Forest
Reserve

chapter 10

NORTH KAUA‘I

What to See:
1. Na Pali Coast State Wilderness Park
2. Hanalei Bay
3. Waiʻoli Huiʻia Church
4. Mission House
5. Limahuli Botanical Garden
6. Na ʻAina Kai Botanical Gardens
7. Kilauea Point National Wildlife Refuge

What to Do:
8. ʻAnini Beach County Park
9. Makua Beach ("Tunnels")
10. KEʻE BEACH ★
11. Hawaiian Surfing Adventures
12. Kalalau Trail
13. Prince Golf Course
14. Princeville Makai Golf Course
15. Princeville Ranch Adventures
16. Silver Falls Ranch
17. Princeville Ranch Stables
18. Kauaʻi Kunana Dairy
19. Haraguchi Rice Mill

Places to Eat & Drink:
20. Kilauea Bakery & Pau Hana
21. Lighthouse Bistro
22. Happy Talk Lounge
23. Bali Hai Restaurant
24. Hanalei Taro & Juice Co.
25. Polynesia Café
26. Hanalei Dolphin Restaurant & Fish Market
27. Postcards Café
28. Tahiti Nui

Where to Shop:
29. Kilauea Sunshine Market
30. Hanalei Farmers Market
31. Kong Lung Center
32. Banana Joe's
33. Ching Young Village Shopping Center
34. Hanalei Dolphin Center

Where to Stay:
35. St. Regis Princeville
36. Westin Princeville Ocean Resort Villas
37. Hanalei North Shore Properties
38. Hanalei Bay Resort

★ *Top Picks*

After all, Hawaii is the best land.

Hawaiian proverb

• SNAPSHOT •

From Kilauea Point in the east to the Na Pali Coast in the west, northern Kaua'i is all about drama. Almost everyone refers to the main road as the Kuhio Highway, which eliminates some confusion. From Hanama'ulu Bay north of Lihu'e until Princeville, it's also known as Route 56. After Princeville, it becomes Route 560. Towering remains of volcanoes stretch to the sea, enfolding some of the most beautiful beaches on the island, especially the sand crescent at Hanalei (of "Puff the Magic Dragon" fame). The planned community of Princeville includes manicured condominiums and amazing golf courses that challenge players to keep their eyes on the ball as well as the view. The cooler upland country is the ideal place for a horseback ride, and the wild Na Pali Coast beckons adventurous hikers and backpackers; the only way in is on foot.

WHAT TO SEE

The words "grandeur" and "majesty" appear frequently in descriptions of Kaua'i's otherworldly ★**NA PALI COAST** *(northwest Kaua'i)* and for good reason. These sheer emerald cliffs (*Na Pali* means "The Cliffs") soar dizzying heights above the Pacific and undulate over 20 miles along the coast. The lush river-cut valleys dotted with fresh-water cascades provided a home for early set-

TOP PICK!

tlers (and for "gone native" nonconformists today). The area is inaccessible by auto, but hiking along trails including the rugged **Kalalau Trail (12)** *(see page 189)* and limited camping are permitted in the **Na Pali Coast State Wilderness Park (1)** *(808-274-3444, www.hawaiistate parks.org/parks/kauai, daily during daylight hours)*. A number of tour operators provide air and sea excursions that allow you to see the cliffs.

It's no wonder **Hanalei Bay (2)** *(off Hwy. 560, Hanalei, west of Princeville)* was featured in the 1958 classic film *South Pacific*; a more perfect picture of paradise may not exist. The creamy crescent of sand (Hanalei means "Crescent Bay"), the turquoise water, and the long walking/fishing pier draw fans from the world over. The view of Hanalei Valley, best seen from the **Hanalei Valley scenic overlook** *(pullout off Kuhio Hwy./Hwy. 56 just beyond the Princeville turnoff)* seems a magical quilt of greens and blues.

American Gothic-style Wai'oli ("joyful water") **Hui'ia Church (3)** *(5-5393A Kuhio Hwy./Rte. 560, Hanalei, 808-826-6253, www.hanaleichurch.org)* offers a Christian service open to all *(Su 10AM, come as you are)*; the choir is famous for its renditions of early Hawaiian hymns. Behind the pretty green church, Hanalei's historic **Mission House (4)** *(5-5373 Kuhio Hwy., Hanalei, 808-245-3202, Tu, Th, Sa 9AM–3PM)* is open for guided tours.

Limahuli Botanical Garden (5) *(5-8291 Kuhio Hwy./Rte. 560, Hanalei, 808-826-1053, http://ntbg.org/gardens/*

limahuli.php, Tu–Sa self-guided tours 9:30AM–4PM, guided tour 10AM, reservations required for guided tour), part of the **National Botanical Gardens** *(see also page 172),* offers guided and unguided walks on a loop trail, steep in some areas. The lush vegetation here was selected by the American Horticultural Society as "Best Natural Botanical Garden" in the United States. **Na'Aina Kai Botanical Gardens (6)** *(4101 Wailapa Rd., Kilauea, 808-828-0525, www.naainakai.com, open by guided tour only Tu–F for visitors 13–up, children's garden tour available for families with children under 13, Orchid House Visitor Center & Gift Shop open M 8AM–2PM, Tu–Th 8AM–5PM, F 8AM–1PM, gardens closed weekends & holidays)* is a 240-acre property filled with themed gardens, including a formal garden with a maze and topiaries, a desert garden, and a children's garden with a rubber tree house and wading pool, plus stands of hardwood trees, a fern-filled canyon, a beach, and more. Sculptures and whimsical statues dot the premises. Guided tours only; reservations recommended. A well-stocked gift shop provides mosquito repellant, but you may wish to bring your own.

On the northernmost tip of the Hawaiian Islands, the U.S. Fish and Wildlife Service's **Kilauea Point National Wildlife Refuge (7)** *(end of Kilauea Rd./Lighthouse Rd. & Hwy. 56, Kilauea, 808-828-1413, www.fws.gov/kilauea point/, daily 10AM–4PM, closed major holidays)* is one of the few refuges open to the public. It offers breathtaking

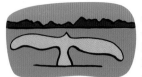

cliff views and an opportunity to visit the 1913 **Kilauea Lighthouse**. The refuge is home to rare and common sea and land birds and unique native plants. Monk seals, spinner dolphins, and whales may be spotted in the Pacific waters below, depending on the season. A Visitor Center offers interpretive dioramas, roving interpreters answer questions, and a Natural History Association bookstore provides further reading.

WHAT TO DO
Beaches:

'Anini Beach County Park (8) *('Anini Rd., Kalihiwai Rd. W., off Hwy. 56, Kilauea, 808-241-4463, www.kauai. gov, open daily)* fronts one of Kaua'i's longest exposed reefs, affording excellent snorkeling in addition to windsurfing and swimming. Facilities include pavilions, picnic tables, comfort stations, and cold showers. Camping by permit *(call 808-241-4460 or visit www.kauai.gov/ visiting/)*. Note: There is some boat traffic here.

Unmarked **Makua Beach** ("Tunnels") (9) *(access via 1 of 2 dirt roads past mile marker 8 on Rte. 560, no facilities, open daily)*, is celebrated for snorkeling and scuba. The name refers to its underwater caves and  crevices. Experienced snorkelers and divers head for the caves; others stay near the reef. Swimming and windsurfing are good here, too, but monitor conditions and watch for folks fishing from boats. Parking is limited, but the beach is less crowded because of it. Don't park on the highway; you'll be ticketed. Some park at **Ha'ena Beach Park** and walk back.

The sunsets are spectacular at ★**KE'E BEACH (10)** (*Ha'ena State Park, Kuhio Hwy./Rte. 560, www.hawaiistateparks.org/parks/ Kauai, open daily*), located at the end of the road. Parking is always a trial here, since the beach is one of the state's most popular, offers restrooms, lifeguards, and showers, serves as the base for the **Kalalau Trail (12)** (*see next page*), and is close to a series of wet and dry caves. Try coming first thing in the morning. The spot has also been the filming location for movies and miniseries, such as *The Thorn Birds* and *Castaway Cowboys*. A jungle path at the end of the beach leads up to an ancient *heiau* (place of worship), an altar dedicated to the hula goddess Laka. Her modern-day students often leave *lei* offerings here. The reef-protected lagoon allows for wonderful swimming and snorkeling during calmer summer months (but always be aware of changing conditions). Note: Do not walk on the coral beds. The practice is not only dangerous (rogue waves can easily take the unaware out to sea), but it also kills the coral.

Watersports:

Hawaiian Surfing Adventures (11) (*Hanalei Beach Park, Hanalei, 808-482-0749, www.hawaiiansurfingadventures. com, first lesson daily 8AM, last lesson 2PM*). The school is

TOP PICK!

the brainchild of native Mitch Alapa, who teaches a basic knowledge of surfing before students set foot in the water. In addition to surfing lessons and safaris, his water safety-licensed instructors teach stand-up paddling and take visitors on outrigger canoe trips up the Hanalei River. Surfboard rentals are also available.

Hiking:

The legendary Na Pali Coast **Kalalau Trail (12)** (*begins at Ke'e Beach, Ha'ena State Park, www.hawaiistateparks. org/hiking*) is a difficult, slippery, muddy track that runs 11 miles. It generally takes six to ten hours to complete—one way. Most hikers limit their experience to the tough two miles to Hanakapi'ai, a primitive camping beach; a two-mile side trail from here leads up to Hanakapi'ai Falls. Day-use hiking permits are required to hike beyond the beach, even if you don't plan to camp. Permits may be obtained from the State Parks office in Lihu'e (*Division of State Parks, 3060 Eiwa St., Rm. 306, Lihu'e, 808-274-3444, www.hawaiistateparks. org*). The trail continues for another nine miles of hills and switchbacks before descending to Kalalau Beach. Your efforts will be rewarded by glimpses of Hawaii's pristine past in the form of seldom-seen valleys, waterfalls, and pools. Notes: Beware of changing ocean conditions before attempting to swim. Beware of falling rocks. There are "gone native" folks who live along the trail, but you may not see them.

Golf:

The community of Princeville boasts two top golf courses designed by Robert Trent Jones, Jr.—the rolling, links-style **Prince Golf Course (13)** *(5-3900 Kuhio Hwy./Rte.560, Princeville, 800-826-1105, www.princeville.com/prince_course.html, daily 6:30AM–6:30PM)* named number one in Hawaii by *Golf Digest* magazine; and the **Princeville Makai Golf Course (14)** *(4080 Lei O Papa Rd., Princeville, 800-826-1105, www.princeville.com/makai_course.html, daily 6:30AM–6:30PM)*, a  27-hole, three-course complex (lakes, ocean, woods) rated among the top 100 in America.

More Activities:

Princeville Ranch Adventures (15) *(5-4280 Kuhio Hwy./Rte. 560, Princeville, 808-826-7669 or 888-955-7669, www.adventureskauai.com, tour times vary, tours by reservation)* offers a four-plus-hour Zip N' Dip Expedition (referred to as "Zip N' Drip" when it's raining) that combines eight zipline crossings over amazing scenery with a suspension bridge crossing and a jungle-pool swim. The excursion includes instruction, lunch, and the care of knowledgeable, safety-certified guides. Other tours available, too.

Romeo, Keiki, Pono, and the other horses of **Silver Falls Ranch (16)** *(2818 Kamoʻokoa Rd., off Kahiliholo Rd., Kilauea, 808-828-6718, www.silverfallsranch.com, ride*

times vary, rides by reservation) carry their riders into some of the most beautiful country in the world. Some rides include stops at mountain pools and waterfalls or a Hawaiian-style picnic. **Princeville Ranch Stables (17)** *(5-4430 Kuhio Hwy./Rte. 560, Princeville, 808-826-6777, www.princevilleranch.com; ride times vary, rides by reservation)* takes visitors on waterfall swim/picnic rides, cattle drive rides, ocean bluff vista rides, or private rides through one of Hawaii's oldest working ranches.

A "micro-dairy" with approximately 20 goats, **Kaua'i Kunana Dairy (18)** *(4552 Kapuna Rd., Kilauea, 808-828-0095, www.kauaikunanadairy.com, farm tours by appointment)* is known for its artisanal cheese, goat milk soaps, and other products, as well as for its organic produce. Listed on the National Register of Historic Places, **Haraguchi Rice Mill (19)** *(5-5070 Kuhio Hwy./Rte. 560, Hanalei, 808-651-3399, guided tours W 10AM, reservations required; informational kiosk & gift shop open to public M–Sa 10AM–5PM)*, the state's only remaining rice mill, is located within the Hanalei National Wildlife Refuge. Hawaii's refuges are seldom open to the public, so this is a rare opportunity to see an area especially set aside for wildlife. The guided tour winds around taro plant ponds (taro is the farm's major crop) that are visited by endangered native birds; the outing includes taro smoothies and picnic lunch.

PLACES TO EAT & DRINK
Where to Eat:

Kilauea Bakery & Pau Hana Pizza (20) ($) *(Kong Lung Center, 2490 Keneke St., Kilauea, 808-828-2020, daily 6:30AM–9PM)* is popular for all types of baked goods and pizza by the slice. The creative menu, live music, and the open-air plantation garden surrounds at **Lighthouse Bistro (21) ($-$$)** *(Kong Lung Center, 2484 Keneke St., Kilauea, 808-828-0480, www.lighthousebistro.com, lunch M–Sa noon–2PM, dinner nightly 5:30PM– 9PM)* get rave reviews; think fresh fish and seafood, steaks, poultry, and locally-grown ingredients served in a variety of ways.

Princeville's **Hanalei Bay Resort (38)** *(5380 Honoiki Rd., Princeville, 808-826-6522, www.hanaleibayresort.com)* offers two newly renovated dining options, the casual **Happy Talk Lounge (22) ($)** *(daily 11AM–10PM)* and North Shore romantic favorite **Bali Hai Restaurant (23) ($-$$)** *(daily 7AM–9:30PM)*. Expect fabulous views and a menu featuring Asian-fusion seafood, meats, poultry, and fresh island produce.

The **Hanalei Taro & Juice Co. (24) ($)** *(5-5070 #A Kuhio Hwy./Rte. 560, Hanalei, 808-826-1059, www.myspace.com/htjc, M–F 10AM–5PM)* stand, located at the **Haraguchi Rice Mill (19)**, serves all things taro: taro coconut *mochi* (rice), taro hummus, *lau lau* rolls and taro smoothies (also know as Kalo Koolers—*kalo* is another pronunciation of *taro*) based on family recipes. Casual **Polynesia Café (25) ($)** *(5-5190 Kuhio Hwy./ Rte.560, Hanalei, 808-826-1999, call for hours, cash only)*, at the Ching Young Village Shopping Center (33), serves plate lunches and sells baked goods. Seating is outdoors on a covered deck or beneath an umbrella. Located on the Hanalei Heritage River, the **Hanalei Dolphin Restaurant & Fish Market (26) ($-$$)** *(Hanalei Dolphin Center, 5-5016 Kuhio Hwy./Rte. 560, Hanalei, 808-826-6113, www.hanaleidolphin.com, restaurant daily 11:30AM–10PM; fish market daily 10AM–7PM)* is a local and visitor favorite for fresh fish, catch-of-the-day entrées, filet mignon, and chicken, as well as riverside cocktails and appetizers. First come, first served, no reservations. Located in a pretty clapboard building on the *mauka* (mountain) side of the road, **Postcards Café (27) ($)** *(5-5075 Kuhio Hwy A, Hanalei, 808-826-1191, www.postcardscafe.com, daily 6PM–9PM)* is renowned for its seafood, vegetarian, and vegan menu.

Bars & Nightlife:

Tahiti Nui (28) ($) *(5-5134 Kuhio Hwy./Rte. 560, Hanalei, 808-826-6277, www.thenui.com, call for hours)* has been around since the 1960s. A casual place to stop for a drink, snack, and great music, it's THE nightspot on the North Shore.

WHERE TO SHOP

For fresh produce and locally made goods, try a colorful farmer's market, such as Kilauea Sunshine Market (29) *(Kilauea Neighborhood Center, Keneke St. off Lighthouse Rd., Kilauea, 808-828-1712, Th 4:30PM)* or the Hanalei Farmers Market (30) *(Hanalei at Waipa, ½ mile west of town, look for signs, Tu 2PM).*

The Kong Lung Center (31) *(2490 Keneke St., Kilauea, 808-828-1822, hours vary by store)* offers a variety of shops that sell everything from fine furnishings and antiques to clothing and candles. Famed anchor retailer **Kong Lung Co.** *(www.konglung.com)* has been serving the community since the late 1800s. Banana Joe's (32) *(5-2719 Kuhio Hwy./Rte. 56, Kilauea, 808-828-1092, www.bananajoekauai.com, M–Sa 9AM–6PM, Su 9AM–5PM)* is an island mainstay. The well-stocked fruit stand is also a good place to stop for smoothies, healthy snacks, and produce. Some swear by the pineapple/banana frosty.

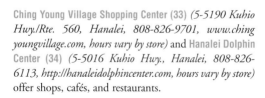

Ching Young Village Shopping Center (33) *(5-5190 Kuhio Hwy./Rte. 560, Hanalei, 808-826-9701, www.ching youngvillage.com, hours vary by store)* and Hanalei Dolphin Center (34) *(5-5016 Kuhio Hwy., Hanalei, 808-826-6113, http://hanaleidolphincenter.com, hours vary by store)* offer shops, cafés, and restaurants.

WHERE TO STAY

Formerly the Princeville Resort, the recently renovated **St. Regis Princeville (35)** **($$$-$$$$)** *(5520 Kahaku Rd., Princeville, 808-826-9644 or 800-325-3580, www.star wood.com/princeville)*, now a Starwood time share property, offers luxuriously appointed accommodations, from mountain/garden rooms to Royal Suites. The recently completed **Westin Princeville Ocean Resort Villas (36)** **($$$$)** *(3838 Wyllie Rd., Princeville, 808-827-8700, www.starwoodvacationownership.com)* offer studios and one- and two-bedroom villas with private *lanais* and all the amenities you'd expect, available for purchase as time shares.

Many rentals, including condos and homes, are handled by private agencies such as **Hanalei North Shore Properties (37)** **($$-$$$$)** *(Princeville Shopping Center, 5-4280 Kuhio Hwy. #2, Hanalei, 808-826-9622 or 800-488-3336, www.kauai-vacation-rentals.com)*. **Hanalei Bay Resort (38)** **($$-$$$$)** *(5380 Honoiki Rd., Princeville, 808-826-6522, www.hanaleibayresort.com)* features privately owned one-, two-, and three-bedroom villas with kitchen facilities. Guests may enjoy the resort's beach access, restaurant, pools, tennis courts, hot tub, and Hawaiian gardens.

Charming **Aloha Plantation B&B (39)** **($)** *(4481 Malulani St., Kilauea, 808-828-1693, 877-658-6977, www.alohaplantation. com)* is an inexpensive option on the north shore. This former plantation manager's house features a room with double bed and bath, a two-bedroom room with bath, and a suite with kitchenette. The property features a courtyard, outdoor kitchen, and vintage Hawaiiana decor. Just steps away from Wainiha Bay, **Hale Hoʻo Maha B&B (40) ($$)** *(7083 Alamihi Rd., Hanalei, 808-826-7083, 800-851-0291, www.aloha.net/~hoomaha)* is built on stilts above the flood zone. An elevator takes guests up to its Pineapple, Guava, Mango, and Papaya suites, as well as to the great room and *lanai*. **Hanalei Inn (41) ($$)** *(5-5468 Kuhio Hwy./Rte.560, Hanalei, 808-826-9333, www.hanaleiinn.com)* offers smallish rooms or studio apartments with kitchens a block from the beach and within walking distance of shops and eateries.

Camping: Na Pali Coast State Wilderness Park (1) offers permit-only camping for experienced backpackers. Special rules apply because the park is so popular. Visit the state parks' Web site *(www.hawaiistateparks. org/camping/permit_napali.cfm)* well in advance of your trip for details. Tips: Bring your own drinking water, pack out your trash, and be aware that water and weather can be extreme. There are restrooms, showers, trash cans, drinking water, and a pay phone in **Haʻena State Park** *(see also page 189)*.

INDEX

NOTES

NOTES

NOTES